Fly Fishing the South Platte River

Fly Fishing the
SOUTH PLATTE
River

ROGER HILL

PRUETT PUBLISHING COMPANY
BOULDER, COLORADO

For information about permission to reproduce selections from this book write to
Permissions, Pruett Publishing Company, 2928 Pearl Street, Boulder, CO 80301.

Library of Congress Cataloging-in-Publication Data

Hill, J. Roger.
  Fly fishing the South Platte River : an angler's guide / J. Roger Hill.
    p.   cm.
  ISBN 0-87108-817-7 : $13.95
    1. Trout fishing—South Platte River (Colo. and Neb.)—Handbooks, manuals, etc.
2. Fly fishing—South Platte River (Colo. and Neb.)—Handbooks, manuals, etc. I. Title.
SH688.U6H55 1991   91-31121
799.1′755—dc20   CIP

Printed in the United States of America
10 9 8 7 6 5 4 3

Book and book cover design by Jody Chapel, Cover to Cover Design
Photographs by Ron Truax

To My Family:

Vicki
Fishing Widow, Beloved Wife

Jeff
Fishing Buddy, Beloved Son

Amanda
Beloved Daughter
Fishing Isn't Everything

Special thanks to Ron Truax for black and white photography.

Contents

Foreword

Finally we have a reliable and comprehensive angling guide to Colorado's famed South Platte River! You have before you the most in-depth book yet written on the always challenging, sometimes infuriating insect hatches found in the South Platte. In *Fly Fishing the South Platte,* Roger Hill, a long-familiar face on the river, has filled a much-needed gap in the "how to" of angling our major western rivers. It is long overdue.

If you have fished the South Platte for years, as I have, you probably had to learn its unusual characteristics by the seat of your pants—as I did. If you have never fished the river before but intend to do so in the near future, this book is a good investment. There's an old saying about fly-fishing success on the South Platte that is not unlike the saying about that big city back East: "If you can make it there you can make it anywhere."

For years I struggled with the complexities of the so-called South Platte method of dead-drift nymphing with a lead weight on the leader. After years of frustration, I finally got quick enough to set the hook in about one-third of the trout to which I present a size 22 Trico emerger. These days I can actually land a few of them on a 7X tippet, but learning that trick took even longer than figuring out how to get a rise. Now Roger Hill has given us the benefit of his years of experience in dealing with such useful South Platte techniques as fishing behind a trout's "blind spot" and presenting pupae and emerger patterns to fish suspended (as South Platte trout do just to piss off fishermen) in several feet of water. He even tells us how to deal with the most exasperating (and frequent) hatch on the river, that of the appropriately named *goddamnedspinneymountaingreenringtailedsonofabitch midge* (Roger's classification—but it fits).

Roger's book will get you started in the right direction. It concentrates on two of the most popular spots on the river, Cheesman Canyon and Spinney Mountain Ranch. He gives a detailed description of the somewhat different hatches and hatch sequences and offers useful tips on presentation and other helpful techniques for each of these somewhat diverse tailwaters. In his introduction, Roger sums up the most common feature of both stretches. "What distinguishes the South Platte from other trout streams," he writes, "is that its dominant aquatic insects are so small." In many ways, that's what this book is all about.

Chapter 10 gives us a look at the imitations for the South Platte as well as detailed tying instructions. There are even suggestions for what to have ready in your fly box at all times when you visit the South Platte.

Chapter 9 is special to me because it deals with one of the most widely known features of the South Platte River, the struggle to prevent the construction of the proposed Two Forks Dam. Roger evokes his love of the river in this chapter and gives us insight into some of the intangibles that keep many of the river's regulars coming back year after year. Certainly the ecological imbalances the dam would have created, not to mention the destruction of what some say is the best trout stream within an hour of a big city in the United States, were enough reason for opposition to the project. But for some of the regulars, there is an added ingredient, the thing that keeps us coming back year after year: tradition. Every year it's talked about; every year it's written about in the outdoor sections of the newspapers. Like other authors writing about the South Platte, Roger Hill transmits that feeling of tradition.

Quite simply, the South Platte is *the* river where many anglers start their season. They have been doing that for something like 140 years now. In fact, the South Platte's angling heritage is so deep that it just might have the oldest tradition of any river in the Rocky Mountain West— which may make it the western equivalent of the Battenkill or the Neversink. For this reason I was thrilled when the publishers asked me to relate a little of that heritage as an introduction to this book. The South Platte is certainly important enough to have history included in a book about it.

As an angling historian, I guess I'm as rare as one of those varieties of big brown mayflies that you see hatching on your favorite stretch of river every ten or twelve years. There aren't many of us, but there are enough. If the angling heritage of the South Platte interests you, read on. If not, turn ahead to Roger's stuff. You can read it straight through, or start by thumbing through it and trying to solve those age-old questions you've had but haven't yet found a logical answer to. Then go fish the South Platte. You'll be part of a tradition that stretches back well over a century.

From the earliest years of white settlement following the discovery of gold in the canyons of the eastern slope of the Colorado Rockies, the South Platte has been used *and* abused. Starting in 1858, with the first settlements, immigrants along the South Platte Trail cut most of the cottonwood trees for fuel at their campsites. In 1867 an irrigation canal was dug on the South Platte to divert water from the river through what became known popularly as "the city ditch." This open canal provided life for the lawns and rows of young elms in frontier Denver.

Upstream from Denver, the forks of the South Platte tumble through the foothill canyons that descend steeply from the high desert valley known as South Park and the higher timberlined peaks beyond, where the river has its origins. Here, before the coming of white settlement, the greenback cutthroat, the only trout native to the drainage, abounded. Almost immediately after the discovery of gold, the river generated an angling interest, and the trout, like the precious water, were exploited both intentionally and unintentionally.

One of the earliest fish stories on record in the Rocky Mountains occurred on February 25, 1861, when frontier Denver's principal newspaper, the *Rocky Mountain News,* reported on a "wagon load of fish" being brought in from the South Platte drainage. The trout were to be sold in an open-air market on Blake Street in the city. "Think of it," marveled the *News,* "fresh fish flowing out of the canyons of the Rocky Mountains."

From that time forward the insidious institution of market fishing became a fixture in the territorial West. In a region of boom-and-bust financial prospects, men often had to turn to other means of earning a living when their mining claims failed. Armed with a few sticks of dynamite, a man could easily "harvest" a few thousand trout for a ready market in an isolated frontier city like Denver. Though the practice was outlawed after Colorado became a state in 1876, the statute was easily and openly evaded. This was a society that bent toward individualism and firmly believed there was no end to the natural resources of the American West.

In July 1884, a marketeer named Peter Cooper was hauled into a Denver courtroom and convicted of dynamiting trout in the South Platte. He was released with a verbal warning from the judge. By the next year, Cooper was at it again farther upstream. This time, because it was his second offense, Cooper was fined the sum of seventy-five dollars.

Sport fishers, too, if I may be so bold as to call them that (actually there were a few good ones), paid little heed to Colorado's bag limits. Catches of hundreds of pounds of trout caught with flies and bamboo rods were not uncommon and were reported in local newspapers. By the late 1870s, a handful of concerned sportsmen declared that fishing in the Platte was finished unless effective laws governing bag limits were passed by the state legislature and enforced rigorously. Mostly, these pleas fell on deaf ears, however, and by the 1880s the greenback cut-throats were pretty much wiped out. By that time, stocking of trout streams had become popular, and imported rainbows started making their appearance in the South Platte.

One of the earliest published fly-fishing adventures in Colorado detailed the catch in 1868 of a large trout, possibly a rainbow, along the North Fork of the South Platte near the present-day town of Pine. That's pretty early for rainbows in the Rockies, but consider the tale. Lewis B. France was Denver's first true sportsman to write professionally about angling in Colorado generally and the South Platte specifically. He traveled upstream by wagon, outfitted for a week-long camping trip during the spring of 1868. In his book, *Rod and Line in Colorado Waters*, now a classic collector's item, France described in a literate Victorian manner how, accoutered in his tweeds and canvas leggings, he took a large South Platte trout on a gray hackle wet fly.

"I struck it rich the first cast," France wrote. "The fraud had barely touched the water before I saw the jaws of a beautiful trout close upon it, and felt his strength at the same instant. . . . As it was, the sport resolved itself into a mere trial of strength between man and fish . . . a three pound trout, the largest I have *ever* caught."

France went on to catch several other trout that day nearly as big. Could they have been rainbows? The biologists inform me that greenback cutthroats seldom exceed thirteen inches. The delicate little natives disappeared early near Colorado's more populous frontier settlements, victims of market harvests and mining waste. Perhaps in more popular fishing waters like the South Platte they were gone within a decade after initial settlement.

Even during the gold rush, the Platte Canyon, which spilled out onto the plains below the town of Morrison, was a very popular playground for Denver anglers. During the 1860s a tortuous winding wagon road took sportsmen like Lewis B. France upriver to productive fishing grounds. But in May 1874, the first tracks of the Denver, South Park & Pacific Railroad were laid, and soon after the main line was pushed through Platte Canyon and eventually up over 9,991-foot Kenosha Pass and into South Park and the headwater forks of the South Platte. The river had to be rechanneled in a dozen different places as miles of roadbed for steel rails were created by blasting forty-foot cuts through solid granite. Much of the fishing along the grade was damaged by silt, rocks, and debris deposited in the river by the dynamite blasts.

The South Park & Pacific was consolidated with other local lines in 1893 to form the Colorado & Southern Railroad. Steam-powered narrow-gauge locomotives carried a host of tourists and fishermen up the canyon weekly until a paved auto road constructed in the 1930s made the trip even faster for Denver anglers.

Throughout the latter decades of the nineteenth century, booster magazines like *The Colorado Tourist* promoted angling in the South Platte by reminding sportsmen that the river was one of the few along the Front Range of the Rockies that had not been ruined by mining effluents. Pioneer newspapers like the *Rocky Mountain News* boasted that the river offered the best fishing in "all the Rockies." Then, as now, accessibility was emphasized. One could take the 8:20 A.M. train out of the city and arrive on the Platte in time to enjoy "four or five hours good fishing and return in time for supper."

One of the favorite trains of the Colorado & Southern Railroad was its Saturday-only "Fisherman Special," which steamed up the canyon as far as the community of Grants and then returned in the evening with its cars full of weary anglers. These so-called "fish trains" were an

institution in Denver angling circles through the early decades of the
twentieth century. They carried not only fishermen, but milk cans of
hatchery-raised trout as well, to be planted in the depleted river.

In 1895 the Colorado & Southern Railroad began stocking 250,000
rainbows annually in the canyon and along the North Fork. In 1899,
to cater mainly to fishermen, the company opened the Kiowa and
Shawnee lodges above the town of Bailey. The lodges, which rivaled
those found on the famed waters of the Catskills, boasted diamond-
paned windows, huge native stone fireplaces, and verandas that "must
be seen to be believed!" according to the *Denver Times*. From 1899
until the Kiowa Lodge was destroyed by fire in 1940, the twin hotels
catered to throngs of knickered anglers who plied the waters of the North
Fork of the South Platte with Leonard and Orvis split-bamboo rods and
silk gut leaders.

The sleepy little village of Deckers was an important destination for
fly fishers in the 1880s, as it is today. Originally called Daffodil, the town
changed its name sometime after the turn of the century to honor one
of the first gold prospectors in the area, Stephen Decker. From the days
of Lewis B. France the little valley at Deckers, with its rustic iron bridge
(still there), had been a favorite with serious anglers. Most would take
the train to South Platte Station, fifteen miles away, and then catch a
stage into the valley. They would camp for several days while casting
gaudy wet fly patterns to the rainbows and browns that now flourished
in the river where greenback cutthroats once thrived.

For years, during the early part of this century, the Colorado fishing
season began on or about the last Saturday in May. The newspapers
inevitably made a big deal of the event, and the South Platte in the
vicinity of Deckers would receive most of the hoopla about the hatchery
trout stocked in the river. "By far the majority [of anglers]," said the
Rocky Mountain News in 1938, "will tramp the trails of the North and
South Forks of the South Platte in the vicinity of Bailey and Deckers
respectively. . . . Literally millions of fish have been planted in these
streams including a large share of . . . one to four pounders."

Newspaper reports after opening day would be accompanied by
pictures of trout stringers containing ten or more fish ranging between
two and six pounds. Even today, despite the fact that Colorado's trout
fishing runs twelve months, many long-time Denver anglers cannot resist

the urge, when they sense the advent of spring's first zephyrs sometime in March, to begin their personal fishing seasons on the South Platte near Deckers. Since the 1970s, however, the put-and-take fishing of past eras has ceased in favor of wild trout management. For much of its length the South Platte is designated either as "gold medal" or "wild trout" water with restricted size and kill limits, and only flies and artificial lures are allowed. Only two fish over sixteen inches may be taken in the river below Deckers, and just upstream in the popular Cheesman Canyon area fishing is catch and release—Colorado's first such designated fishery (as of 1976).

By the end of World War I a genuine South Platte tradition had started to take shape, a highly personal, unspoken love that went beyond the mere urge to get out and "fish Deckers" on opening day. To preserve both that tradition and a short stretch of water that was receiving increasing use, a group of avid fly fishers followed examples set by their forefathers on eastern waters when they decided to purchase exclusive fishing rights to a portion of the river. In February 1921, sixty of the most prominent businessmen in Colorado founded the Wigwam Club. Together they puchased Gill's old resort in the canyon near Deckers for $16,000. Headed by Earl G. Bartels along with eight other directors, the Wigwam Club turned its modest eight acres into one of the choicest private fishing clubs in the West.

By 1928 the club was stocking 200,000 fingerling trout each April into the South Platte from its private hatchery. Although the West was not yet ready for catch-and-release fishing, the club strictly enforced bag limits. They voluntarily curtailed fishing hours, limiting angling to daylight hours only, and required all members to release any trout under eight inches. In addition, they restricted angling to fly fishing only. To be sure, by the standards of the 1990s, these measures seem puny. But according to the ethics of the 1920s, whereby a fisherman measured the success of a trip by how successfully his Kodak Brownie captured the image of his bulging wicker creel, the rules were progressive.

Although the private club concept of purchasing stream rights for the purpose of regulating trout resources had been widespread in the East since the Civil War, the Wigwam Club was one of the few such organizations in the West to take up the cause in the face of expanding and exploiting populations.

The exclusiveness of the Wigwam Club, however, did not sit well with many individualistic westerners, who detested regulation of anything in any form. The club's efforts, nevertheless, paid off, at least for its members. By the 1930s Denver newspapers were reporting catches of huge rainbows by Wigwam anglers. For years, Frederick G. Bonfils, publisher of the *Denver Post,* held the record with a trout of eight and three-quarters pounds. Bonfils's trout, caught May 27, 1932, was a rainbow measuring twenty-seven and one-fourth inches. In September 1938, in one day, an angler named Cliff Welch, using a Rio Grande King, landed three trout of three, six, and seven pounds, respectively, on club property.

Cliff Welch is credited by some with developing the so-called Platte rig, the familiar technique of fishing a single nymph weighted down with split shot or a twist of a thin lead strip on a fairly short leader. Although this method of getting a nymph or wet fly down to bottom was undoubtedly utilized by anglers nationwide at an early date (they used little pieces of buckshot slit with a hunting knife), in the Rockies it is particularly associated with the South Platte. The method requires the concentration of a good pointing dog and the eyes of an eagle, but it has gained much favor among anglers who are skilled at such things.

The story goes that Cliff Welch, a Wigwam member in good standing, was fishing the club property one fine August day in 1935. He was setting the hook in one large rainbow after another while his companions couldn't buy a strike. When asked what he was using, Welch produced a March Brown Nymph tied to the end of a nine-foot leader with a split shot attached above the fly. Club officials were furious. They demanded that Welch give up the practice or be censured from the Wigwam Club, as using weight was not considered proper fly fishing. Rumor has it that he gave it up—but a tradition was born just the same.

Welch's choice of fly, a March Brown, reflected a basic truth about fly pattern development on the South Platte—dull and subdued. Back in 1868, during the days of large gaudy wet flies, Lewis B. France used a "gray hackle" wet fly with peacock body to catch his big trout. Gray, olive, and brown, with lots of peacock herl, was the standard on the river. When Mary Orvis Marbury compiled her angling classic, *Favorite Flies and Their Histories,* published in 1892, she requested fly fishers from across the nation to write to her and identify the flies they found most successful in their respective states. Over 200 anglers responded, including M. D. Byerly of Alma, Colorado, near the headwaters of the South Platte. Byerly identified the Royal Coachman, perhaps the most colorful fly to be used on the river in those days, as an all-time favorite. Others from Colorado concluded that the peacock-bodied Coachman was the top fly for catching trout in the streams of the state (including the South Platte).

Little changed from the Victorian era during the early decades of the twentieth century except that dry fly fishing gained in popularity on the South Platte, as it did throughout America. Even then patterns remained subdued. During the 1930s a pattern known as the Betty McNall fly was popular among members of the Wigwam Club. The dry fly resembled a Royal Coachman except that the wings were tied with deer hair. Indeed, the fly appears to be an independent regional version of the famous Royal Wulff developed in the East by Lee Wulff.

Today, fly patterns have remained subdued, and exact imitation has, for many, become the key to success. As Roger Hill shows, small No-Hackles or Paraduns and floating nymphs are popular. Midges are standard both dry and in their larval and pupal form. Tricos also test the angler. Pheasant Tails and gold-ribbed Hare's Ears, in very small sizes, are popular. One pattern in more modern times has come to be particularly identified with the South Platte. The Brassie Nymph, tied in very small sizes, consists of fine gold or copper wire tied on with a dubbing of muskrat for a thorax. The simple fly, credited by Terry Hallekson in his book, *Popular Fly Patterns,* to Gene Lynch of Colorado Springs, imitates a variety of tiny nymphs found in the South Platte. Weighted with lead about a foot up the leader, in the Cliff Welch manner, the fly has gained a reputation for tricking the finicky brown trout in Cheesman Canyon near Deckers.

One South Platte regular, Bill Phillipson, established a reputation for himself as an innovator and craftsman of fine bamboo fly rods. A Swedish immigrant, Phillipson came to the United States at age eighteen and went to work for the Granger Rod Company in Denver in 1925. Phillipson went into business for himself in 1946. At the height of production, the Phillipson Rod Company produced only 8,000 to 10,000 rods annually. But what fine (yet affordable) rods they were!

Phillipson himself designed and perfected a new type of machine for cutting bamboo strips. He also made advances with the difficult impregnation process. Phillipson rods were soaked in resin only after the six bamboo strips had been glued up into a rod blank. In this way, the resin did not penetrate into the pithy interior of the blank. The result was a moisture-proofed rod of extreme durability for western conditions, yet light enough in weight to maintain the equivalent line weights of a similar-sized nonimpregnated fly rod.

Today, Phillipson bamboo rods are relatively affordable collector's items, costing about as much as a high-quality graphite rod. A good one is still a good choice for the South Platte (for which it was undoubtedly designed four decades ago). A six-weight rod has good power for its size and yet has the potential to drop a delicate #20 Blue-Winged Olive on a low, clear October pool without as much as a dimple.

After his retirement and until his death in 1987, Bill Phillipson frequently could be seen prowling the banks of the South Platte with a Stetson on his head, his eyeglasses reflecting the sunlight. He was as good an angler as he was a rod maker. He had the almost uncanny ability to strike one big rainbow or brown after another while others on the river got a lot of exercise flexing their casting arms. The regulars on the river, and the fly fishing fraternity in general, will sorely miss him.

Perhaps, as Roger Hill tells us in Chapter 9, the South Platte is most famous today because of the fight over the proposed Two Forks Dam. The massive project, which first started making headlines as early as the 1960s, would have flooded about thirteen miles of prime fishing water along the North and South forks of the river, including the historic Deckers area. More than a century of fly-fishing tradition would have been inundated under a reservoir that would have adversely affected wildlife populations as far downstream as western Nebraska.

Concerned anglers opposed to Two Forks have been engaging in the same role acted out by a generation of western anglers almost a century before them toward proposals to dam the South Platte. Outcries of protest are nothing new. On September 17, 1899, an editorial in the *Denver Times* proclaimed that a project to dam the Platte Canyon would "destroy the stream for trout fishing."

In 1900 the Denver Union Water Company started building the Cheesman Dam anyway. No sooner had the project been completed in 1905 than observers began to question its capacity to provide adequately for the future water needs of Denver. Since Cheesman, the South Platte has had her waters impounded by Eleven Mile, Antero, Chatfield, and Spinney Mountain reservoirs and several other lakes in the tributaries.

These dams have been both a curse and a blessing to anglers. Although some stretches of the river were obviously lost, productive tailwater fisheries in Cheesman Canyon and between Spinney Mountain and Eleven Mile reservoirs (the subject of this book) were created. For many an angler, the challenge of fishing for the wary brown trout in Cheesman Canyon is one of the most sought-after experiences on the South Platte, and, as Roger Hill will show, it is one that can be enjoyed most days of the year. The river below Spinney Dam has produced a trophy fishery that just might equal that of any tailwater fishery in the nation. Rainbows running up from Eleven Mile Reservoir during the spring average around fifteen inches, and there are enough fish in the twenty-inch-plus category to keep anglers coming back regularly.

Since 1990, a total of only eighty trout may be taken annually on a short stretch of river below Spinney. A drawing held in December determines who will get the eighty permits, and each successful applicant may keep one fish of any size. The rest of the fishing is strictly catch and release with only flies and artificial lures.

The rainbows in this section of the South Platte are among the most beautifully colored trout I have ever encountered, although there are anglers who would argue in favor of the electrically hued fish around Deckers. Above Spinney Mountain Reservoir, there is a respectable run of fall browns and spring cutthroats during years when there is sufficient water in the river at the inlet to permit their spawning migration.

The endurance of the South Platte River as a quality trout fishery is a triumph against the odds, considering its proximity to a major urban center. There is a basic misconception about the West that because of its vast amount of space, comparatively low populations, a perceived emphasis on so-called "natural" living, and an overall excellent quality of life, the trout streams, therefore, must have remained unspoiled. In truth, westerners historically have been among the worst abusers of their natural resources. The very abundance of space and lack of crowded human populations created the illusion that resources were inexhaustible. To conquer the land, harness its power, and put it to work was encouraged; it was the *right* of the pioneer. Water, however, was always scarce and precious, and it still is. Our forefathers here in the Rockies fought each other for the right to either possess it privately or exploit it unmercifully on an equal basis.

Unregulated in its early years, the South Platte suffered heavy mistreatment. Its native cutthroats were dynamited for profit to feed a rapidly expanding human population. It was dewatered from the start for irrigation. Finally, it was dammed for the future. Yet in the decade of the 1980s, it emerged triumphant despite efforts to change and obliterate it. It has even survived the most politicized environmental battle in history and, thus, once again endured the ages. On occasion, as in the East, it took the efforts of private citizens and exclusive clubs to preserve and enhance it, efforts that were hardly part of the "pioneer way."

Today, you and I still may cast a fly to a wild trout in the "holy water" of Cheesman Canyon. It takes us only a few hours to cover the same ground that our ancestors took a week to traverse by horse and buckboard in pursuit of their sport. Up in the extreme headwater tributaries of the South Platte drainage, in Rocky Mountain National Park, the greenback cutthroat is making a comeback under watchful management. Anglers who start their season near Deckers are doing no less than participating in a tradition that is now over 130 years old. Who knows, next spring when the Blue-Winged Olive hatch comes off in "the Canyon," one or two of these guys might even see the ghost of Lewis B. France fishing alongside of them.

John Monnett, Author of *Cutthroat and Campfire Tales: The Fly Fishing Heritage of the West.*

Preface

As no man is born an artist, so no man is born an angler.
—Isaak Walton, 1593-1683

This guide is the instruction manual I wish I had had when I was learning to fish the South Platte. When I needed it most, it would have been over my head. A lot of it should be over your head as well if it is to benefit you as you struggle to learn what I believe to be one of America's most difficult yet most rewarding trout streams. As you fish the Platte and observe trout and insects, some of the situations discussed here will make more sense to you. As your understanding of the river grows, so will the number of trout you release. You should supplement my information with some continued reading of aquatic entomology; I particularly recommend Gary Borger's two books, *Naturals: A Guide to Food Organisms of the Trout* and *Nymphing: A Basic Book*. Pay particular attention to his discussions of the trout's window and the mirror. You must understand both if you are to become proficient on the Platte.

The information I offer assumes that you have mastered the basics of fly fishing using both nymphs and dry flies and that you know the most basic aquatic entomology and can tie simple flies. I also assume that you want to catch more than a few trout per day in the catch-and-release areas of the South Platte River, or you wouldn't have read this far. I hope to help you get from a few fish per day up to perhaps fifteen on a good summer day and to help you recognize and meet some of the difficult situations that really aren't so difficult once you understand them. I will not offer a compendium of every fly known to have taken more than two trout there, nor a rock-by-rock description of the river, nor any discussions of the physics of fly casting. If you're looking for entertainment or just good fishing literature, I recommend John Gierach. All you will find here is some basic information about bugs and such; a minimal set of simple, effective flies; and an explanation of why, when, and how to fish them. This book is strictly "how to," and I offer no apologies for that.

I struggled to learn the South Platte at a time when there wasn't a fly shop in Colorado Springs and I didn't know a soul who fly fished. In my first dozen trips to Cheesman Canyon I caught perhaps six trout. When a more successful fisherman there explained to me that I needed light tippet (6X), I had to drive to Denver to find it. The only advice I could find came from fishermen on the stream. I learned the stream by reading books on entomology, by seining it, by keeping an aquarium of its bugs, and by asking other fishermen for advice. A lot of what I learned about the river is the result of trial and error, which is a thorough but painfully slow way to learn. There are shortcuts that will save you years of struggle and, I hope, allow you to enjoy the Platte without suffering years of frustration if you're too shy to ask others for help.

The methods and flies I present here are all very simple—and they work. I have shown them to others, and they work for them, too. There is absolutely nothing complicated about learning to fish the Platte, but you must resolve to meet the trout on their own terms, for what they demand is not negotiable. You must be prepared to fish with stealth, often on your knees, and with small flies and light tippet most of the time. If you're willing to do that, the rest is easy.

The word "easy" must be interpreted in a fly-fishing context. Fly fishing is a sport of attention to detail. Although the individual activities of fly fishing are indeed easy, it is the whole rather than the sum of the parts that counts. You must do a number of easy tasks well and simultaneously. You can't do half the tasks right and expect to catch half as many trout as you would if you did everything right. Something as simple as adding another foot of tippet may be the difference between success and failure. If you do everything right most of the time, you will probably catch five times as many trout as you would by doing half of your fishing tasks correctly. Attention to detail produces a synergism. When it all comes together for you, catching trout in the Platte can be pretty easy.

I don't believe anything in this guide is original; every fly pattern and every technique came from somewhere else. I hope that this assembly of the ideas of others will shorten the time it takes you to become proficient on the Platte. Not surprisingly, among those who have fought the hardest to save the Platte are those who fish it successfully. The greatest thanks I can offer those generous gentlemen who helped me become a good fisherman is to help you fish the Platte successfully, in the hope that you will help defend it for them. Your purchase of this guide will help Trout Unlimited in its efforts to protect the South Platte, and for that, I thank you.

1 Introduction

The areas of the South Platte of greatest interest to trout fishermen are the three miles immediately below Spinney Reservoir and the ten miles or so below Cheesman Dam. These tailwater areas offer controlled flows, excellent water chemistry, and the ideal temperature conditions for both trout and the aquatic life forms upon which they feed. That they produce lots of big fish and attract lots of fishermen is to be expected. Fishing pressure and catch-and-release regulations have produced trout that are demanding on an easy day and maddening on a difficult one. Success on those difficult days is what identifies the skilled fisherman. Typically, the difficult days are marked by low water, good insect hatches, and selective feeding behavior by the trout. Trout of the South Platte do not confine their selective behavior to surface feeding alone; nymph fishing can be quite challenging during periods when there isn't a rising trout or insect in sight. To fish the Platte successfully with consistency you must be able to fish either dries or nymphs with equal facility and to move from one method to the other quickly.

The trout of the South Platte, just like the trout of any other stream, feed on mayflies, midges, caddis flies, stone flies, scuds, aquatic earthworms, and the other usual insect life. What distinguishes the South Platte from other trout streams is that its dominant aquatic insects are so small. There are many species of large aquatic insects in the Platte—such as golden stonefly nymphs in Cheesman Canyon, which are two inches long—but not very many individuals. A few of these large nymphs can be found in turbulent waters, but just upstream may be a riffle in which the bottom is covered with millions (maybe billions) of midge pupae about one-quarter inch long. The trout of the Platte grow fat and

1

particular on a diet dominated by such minutae.

The newcomer to the Platte may find this information disheartening, but it has its positive side: I can tie a half-dozen nymphs to imitate a midge pupa in the time it takes to tie a single stone fly nymph. Muskrat fur on a size 24 hook may be all the trout demand. Furthermore, the trout aren't concerned with the fine details of small insects. Trout feeding selectively on small insects are much easier to catch than those feeding selectively on large ones. I've had many days when I caught obscene numbers of trout by fishing exclusively with size 24 flies. On the other hand, I have shown the trout of the Frying Pan River every Green Drake imitation known to man in four sizes and five colors during my annual visits to fish that hatch. I regularly have forty or so trout come up to inspect my imitations of that large insect, yet I have never caught more than a dozen trout on the surface during the four hours the hatch normally lasts.

The Spinney Mountain Ranch and Cheesman Canyon sections of the Platte are quite different in character but similar in their dominant insects and aquatic life. Rainbow trout are the dominant trout species in both sections and are on the average larger than the browns in both sections. The browns you do catch in the Spinney section will generally be larger and better conditioned than those in the Cheesman Canyon section. The Spinney section is a meadow stream with relatively little variation in the character of the bottom and gradual variations in depth. In Cheesman Canyon, however, you can step from water six inches deep into holes ten feet deep! The Canyon section is on the average deeper and faster than the Spinney section, and trout are less likely to rise. Over the course of a year, a skilled angler fishing the Canyon will generally catch most of his trout on nymphs. At Spinney, he will catch most of his fish on dry flies.

A second significant difference between the Spinney and the Cheesman sections is that Cheesman Reservoir is much deeper than Spinney Reservoir and hence the water in Cheesman Canyon warms later than that below Spinney Reservoir. In addition, flow from Cheesman Dam is often erratic, going from 30 cfs one day to 400 cfs the next. This changing flow has the effect of making hatch dates less predictable than they are for the Spinney area. The relatively cooler water also makes the hatches of a given insect occur later in Cheesman

Canyon. These differences are of benefit to the fishermen: when one section is not fishing well the other invariably is.

Learning to fish the Platte is in large measure learning about what, when, and how the trout eat. Much of this knowledge involves the hatching of the various insects and the selective response of the trout to such hatches. Hatches may occur during perhaps 10 percent of your fishing time, but they cause the most difficulty for most fishermen. To fish successfully when there is no hatch requires that you know a considerable amount about the insects and other food and the yearly timing of the hatches.

During periods when no insects are hatching, trout will still be on the lookout for either the adult or nymphal forms of the insects that have been hatching recently. Trout on the Frying Pan will still take a Green Drake imitation for several weeks after that hatch is over for the year. Trout do remember what certain foods look like for a long time after a hatch ends, and they are very likely to take imitations of food items they have eaten recently. Thus, about 90 percent of this guide is devoted to explaining what is going on 10 percent of the time, so that you will be prepared to have fun responding to the demands of the Platte during 100 percent of your time on stream.

2 Comments on Equipment

Fly Rods

Fly rods are a very personal piece of equipment. I'd sooner tell a fellow fisherman what I think of his favorite hunting dog (or even his girlfriend!) and suffer the consequences than tell him what I really think of his new fly rod. I will tell you what I like in fly rods for the South Platte, and why. I use a nine-foot, four-weight rod of conventional graphite with a slow action. The new high-tech graphites represent an incredible advance of the state of the art for those attempting to fish the far bank of the Columbia River, but for those of us for whom a thirty-foot cast is a long one, they don't offer much. When I cast such rods, I have a propensity to splash the fly and leader on the water and spook the trout; stiffness (or "fast action") in a fly rod is hard for me to control. More important, the stiffness of such rods means that I break off far too many trout while setting the hook with light tippet. With my "soft action" rods, I don't break off any trout while fishing 6X tippet and usually only one or two per year with 7X tippet.

The nine-foot rod length is a compromise. I would prefer a ten-foot rod if it weren't so heavy and tiring to cast. I like to reach a considerable distance across currents while fishing nymphs and to be able to dap a dry fly on the water while a good distance away from a trout. Nine feet is a workable length for my style of fishing, which is more pragmatic than stylish. For windy conditions, I do fish a fast action five-weight that gives me a better chance of getting the fly where I want it.

5

Leaders

I do most of my fishing with a hand-tied leader that has all of its knots painted fluorescent orange. This leader makes nymph fishing considerably easier because the knots are visible under water, thus making the strike to a nymph more apparent. My favorite one is tied as follows:

Length	Diameter
36″	.022″
18″	.020″
12″	.017″
6″	.015″, .012″, and .010″
12″	.007″ (loop at end)

I then add 18–36 inches of appropriate tippet, attached with a loop-to-loop connection. You can fish dries as well as nymphs with this leader. I remove my painted knot leaders only to fish to the most skittish of trout, typically holding in very quiet water. The loop knot I use is sketched here:

1.

Loop tippet over itself.

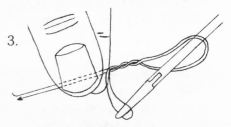

3.

Pull first loop through double-strand loop.

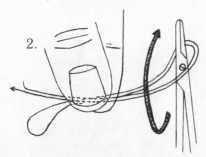

2.

Bring loop over itself again to create another loop with two strands. Insert hemostats in second loop from below. Twist three turns clockwise.

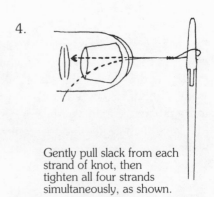

4.

Gently pull slack from each strand of knot, then tighten all four strands simultaneously, as shown.

Insert your hemostats in the double loop, twist three times in a clockwise direction, and then pull the single loop through with the hemostats before tightening all four strands simultaneously. This knot is much stronger than either perfection or surgeon's loops for fine tippets.

Tie the loop itself several inches long. Hang the leader by the loop in the 4X (.007 ″) section and paint the knots with Dave's Flexament. Follow with flat white enamel of the type used on plastic model airplanes, then fluorescent orange enamel, and then another drop of Flexament (allowing to dry between each application). Use a match stick for painting. This leader will improve your nymphing more than any other trick I have found. When fishing nymphs, put the lead on the loop portion of the tippet. The signal for the strike to a nymph is any *change* in the motion of the knots as they drift through the water. You may also spot takes of small dries by the motion of the painted leader knots when you cannot see your fly on choppy water.

Hooks

Most of your imitations of South Platte insects will be tied on small hooks, and for small sizes I find the additional expense of Tiemco hooks to be money well spent. Use smooth-jawed hemostats to remove small flies from the box and hold flies as you tie them to your tippet. You can also flatten the barb with them, making release of either trout or your index finger easier. I have to remove a hook from my hide about once every two days of fishing, so I strongly recommend barbless hooks. If anything, you will land more trout while fishing barbless hooks because they set so easily that many trout will hook themselves before you even realize you've had a strike. Barbless hooks are much easier on the trout because of the reduced handling necessary to remove the hook. If you insist on fishing barbed flies you must be prepared to spend time tying many additional flies. If you have to grasp a fly with hemostats to remove it, it will quickly disintegrate. This is particularly true for tiny barbed flies, which are almost impossible to remove without hemostats. In summary, if you leave the barbs on tiny flies, tie a lot of them. If you leave the barbs on large flies, mentally rehearse how you will remove one from your right thumb while using only your mouth and left hand. Barbless hooks are easier on both you and the trout.

Seine

Build a seine by stapling a two-by-three-feet piece of fiberglass screen to two half-inch dowel rods. Seine the river every time you fish until you know the river very well. By doing this you will spot the insects likely to hatch that day and know the appropriate patterns and sizes required to match the hatch. You will also adapt patterns to match the nymphs you observe. You can't help but learn more aquatic entomology just from looking at the immature nymphs and other life forms you find. Seining the river regularly will make you a better fisherman.

Kneepads

Another important piece of equipment will be found not in an Orvis catalog but in a tradesman's supply store. Buy a pair of carpet layer's kneepads and use them. The ones with hard plastic shells are best.

Waders

Don't try to fish the Platte in hip boots. You'll end up wet and cold (believe me, I know!).

Backpack

You will enjoy your days in the Canyon much more if you carry your gear into the area in a frame-type backpack. If you walk in in chest-waders you will be wringing wet when you start fishing and wringing wet, tired, and smelly by the time you get back to your car (believe me, I know!).

3 Tips on Presentation

The single most important thing to understand before you can master the South Platte is that it is not difficult to catch trout you haven't spooked, and it is impossible to catch those you have. The trout of the Platte see great numbers of fishermen and are remarkably tolerant of their presence. When they know a human is present, they may continue to feed, but they are much more guarded and more likely to be very particular about what they eat, taking only organisms upon which they had been feeding prior to the fisherman's arrival. If they are unaware of your arrival, however, they may take almost anything.

The ability to see trout is essential if you are serious about mastering the Platte or any other trout river. In order to see any object, you must see the light reflected by it. Other light not reflected from the object makes this more difficult. (Why do you shield your eyes when trying to see something between your eyes and the sun?) A hat and polaroid sunglasses are your most important pieces of equipment. Together they improve the signal-to-noise ratio for your fish detector, your eyes. The signal in this case is light reflected from the trout. The noise is other light reaching your eye that is not reflected from the trout. The polaroids filter out much of the light that has been reflected from the water's surface, which is noise since it hasn't been reflected by the trout. The majority of the noise is direct sunlight, which can be blocked by a hat. With polaroids and a hat you can see trout even in broken water. All you have to do is focus on the bottom and watch for perhaps thirty seconds. In turbulent water you may have to wait for a small area of flat water to pass by, but if trout are there you will eventually see them. This brings us to the second most important thing to understand before

11

you can master the Platte: *It is easier to catch trout if you fish where the trout are rather than where they aren't.*

Many fishermen are skeptical of their ability to see trout if they have not previously tried to develop this skill. I emphasize that it is an acquired skill and not a gift of genetics. Some summer afternoon when fishing is slow, put your rod and vest in the car and spend your afternoon sitting on the banks, looking for trout in various types of water. Get on your hands and knees and crawl upstream along the bank, spotting trout and seeing how close you can get to them before they are spooked. You'll be a better fisherman before the evening fishing begins.

The third most important thing to understand before you start to learn the Platte is that *all trout have a blind spot in their rearview mirrors;* if you are just a short distance directly behind them, they can't see you. As long as you wade quietly and don't get too close to them, trout directly upstream from you will never know you're there.

How close you can get to the trout depends upon how far you extend above the water's surface. If you stay below the line radiating out from the trout at approximately ten degrees' elevation from the water's surface, the trout cannot see you. If you're six feet tall and standing in three feet of water, only three feet of you is available to be above that line, and you can get within about twenty feet of the trout without it being able to see you. If you are standing on a three-foot bank, you extend to nine feet above the water's surface, and you must be more than fifty feet away to be invisible to the trout! A lot of the time, I am only two feet or less above the water. I fish on my knees in water up to two feet deep and get very close to the trout, typically within fifteen to twenty feet, without them having any idea that I'm there. If you choose to appear nine feet tall, that hat I insist you wear should be a fluorescent orange dunce cap. If you are going to fish from the bank, at least sit down.

One of my fishing friends, Dick Storey, has raised staying low to an art form. He finds a submerged rock in the river, sits down on it, and doesn't move until he has caught every trout within an easy cast. He is sometimes on the same rock for several hours. With just a little effort and care on your part, you can spend almost all of your fishing time casting short distances to visible trout that are totally unaware of your presence.

Staying low and getting close to the trout has other benefits. I get many more presentations because little false casting is required. Furthermore, I can put a fly within six inches of where I want it with a twenty-foot cast. I can't get within two feet if I have to cast forty feet. Quite often I will crawl to within ten feet behind a large trout holding in an eddy along the bank and simply reach forward with the rod and dap the fly onto its eddy. In Cheesman Canyon I use the large rocks to hide behind as I fish to nearby trout. I've caught a lot of big trout simply by being willing to sneak up on them, even if it meant getting my hands dirty.

There will be many occasions while fishing dry flies when you can stand and fish any way you want without spooking the trout. If you're fishing in the riffles, the trout do not have an undistorted view of you, and as long as you stay a reasonable distance from them and move slowly, you can cast any direction you wish. If you can't fish upstream in flat water, however, it is important to stay low. In waist-deep water, I spread my feet wide apart and bend over while casting to trout on the opposite bank. If the water is shallow enough, I may approach the trout on my knees from a position quartering upstream. Even if you cast very well at long distances, it is difficult to fish a dry fly effectively across a multitude of currents. The continual gathering and lengthening of line and false casting takes up valuable time when your fly should be on the water. You will catch more trout if you stay as low as possible and get as close to the trout as you can without spooking it.

In summary, whenever practical, wade and fish directly upstream to trout you can see but that can't see you. This is as important for nymphing as for dry-fly presentation. It isn't always possible or even desirable to fish straight upstream, particularly if you have to stand in eight feet of water to do so. Sometimes complex currents, water depth, very low flow, or terrain dictate that the best approach is from the side or upstream from the trout.

Most fishermen you see fishing a nymph do so from a position about ten feet to the side of the trout. This works just fine in broken water in which the trout's view of the outside world is greatly distorted by the choppy water surface. It doesn't work at all if the trout is in the slick behind a rock where it has a clear view of the fisherman. I do 90 percent of my nymph fishing straight upstream, but there are still times when I do fish from the side. Use several strike indicators spread along your leader or a painted knot leader if you have difficulty detecting a strike when fishing a nymph upstream.

Fishing a nymph straight upstream does not work well in either deep or fast water because you cannot get your nymph to the bottom quickly. For these situations stand to the side of the trout, cast your nymph about fifteen feet upstream of the trout, and immediately mend your line so that it lies on the surface upstream of where the nymph entered the water. The upstream mend will put the leader into a position where it actually pushes the nymph under and allows it to sink quickly. After the nymph drifts to a position a few feet upstream of the trout, raise your rod tip to hold all but the leader off the water. This will result in a drag-free drift of the nymph along the bottom where the trout will most likely be feeding.

When you must stand to the side to fish a nymph, your approach to the trout is critical to your success. Be very careful to pick up your feet so that you don't turn over rocks as you slowly wade into position. Once you are in position, *do not move your feet.* If at all possible, position yourself so that there is an area of broken water between you and the trout.

Nymph fishing requires that you continually adjust the weight on your leader to compensate for changing water conditions (speed and depth) and to stay where the trout are feeding. Most of the time they will be feeding right on the bottom, and that is where your nymph must be if you are to succeed. If you drop even a tiny split shot into fast water it will sink to the bottom, somewhere downstream of where you dropped it, and stay there. If you attach this same shot to a leader attached to a floating line and cast it upstream in that same fast water, it will never hit the bottom, let alone carry a nymph down with it. Drag on the floating line and leader by the faster currents at the surface balances the pull of gravity on the dense lead. To get a nymph to the bottom, the lead must be heavy enough to overcome the upward pull due to the drag on the leader and floating line. What this means to you is that the amount of lead must be adjusted to such a weight that it (the lead) is pulled along the bottom by drag on the leader and floating line at the speed of the current *on the bottom.* Too much lead will sink to the bottom and stop; too little will never reach the bottom. You must be willing to adjust your lead every time conditions call for it, even if you have taken only one step to get to a new spot.

Visual clues are also important when nymphing, particularly when you are fishing a nymph to several visible trout. If any one of them moves or flashes while your nymph appears to be anywhere within five feet of that trout, tighten the line. The trout moved for a reason, which may be to take your nymph. It's easy enough to find out. When you do tighten the line while nymphing do it gently, for several reasons. First, if you tighten rapidly you will foul hook large numbers of trout. Second, you will also break off many trout that have taken your nymphs. Third, the lead on your leader will spin in the water if pulled through the water rapidly, and you will spend a lot of time replacing twisted tippets. (The last consideration is the reason I use split shot rather than twist-on lead while nymphing; it doesn't spin as readily as you pick up your nymph to cast again.) Further, you should bear in mind that your nymph will invariably be upstream of where you think it is due to the surface currents being faster than those on the bottom. You may think your nymph has passed a trout that moved; most likely it has not.

I am continually amused by fishermen and the things that bedevil them. I regularly encounter competent fishermen catching a few trout on nymphs during a hatch of small flies. Every trout in the river may be looking up to feed, but these fishermen refuse to fish with small dry flies because they can't see them on the water. They somehow hook fish without seeing them take a nymph, yet they are puzzled about what to do when they can't see a small dry on the surface. Compared to the inhalation of a nymph, a trout rising anywhere in this hemisphere is a signal as loud as a Klaxon horn that a tiny dry fly may be in its mouth! If there is any doubt at all, tighten the line and find out. If you do it gently you won't spook trout; at the worst, you'll have to cast again. As long as the trout can see your fly, you don't need to.

If you still insist that you must see a small dry in order to fish it, use a fly you can see as a strike indicator. Tie on a size 18 Parachute Adams, then attach an 18-inch length of appropriate tippet to its eye and tie the small fly to it. I sometimes try this method in mayfly and caddis hatches, using the adult imitation of the natural insect as the strike indicator and the corresponding nymph or emerger on the dropper. Whichever the trout wants, you've offered it.

If you fished the South Platte every day for a year, you would discover that you used six spools of 6X tippet for every spool of anything else. Use 6X tippet for fly sizes 18-24. Use 5X for size 16, 7X for sizes 26-28, and 4X for anything size 14 or larger. The Platte's reputation for requiring light tippet exists not because the trout are leader-shy but because they require a drag-free drift that is obtainable only if the tippet isn't large enough to affect the motion of the (small) flies required. There will be some occasions when fishing size 22-24 flies when you will prefer 7X tippet, but not very many of them.

The only thing the trout of the South Platte demand of your presentation is perfection. Anything less isn't good enough for them. Fortunately, the Platte has many more than one trout, and you usually get more than one try at each of them. If you get to the point where one-fourth of your presentations are perfect, you'll be among the best fishermen on the river.

Let's suppose that you have presented the right fly to the trout with a presentation that is, in a word, perfect. The trout is completely fooled and takes your fly. What now? What you do now is pause to recite: *"The trout is not a bass and a small fly is not a bass plug and you don't set the hook the way those bass fishermen do on TV!"* After you've repeated every word of that, smoothly and *gently* lift the rod until you just feel the trout, then drop the rod tip to give it a bit of slack before it begins to fight. Let the trout have its first run without touching the reel. If you hooked it in fast water, be ready to get on the bank and chase it downstream to minimize pressure on that light tippet. After its first run, keep a small amount of pressure on the trout, but let it go against the drag on the reel only if it runs again. If it jumps, quickly drop the tip of the rod, then raise it again after it hits the water. After its first few runs you should be able to bring the trout in to gently revive and release it, while other envious fishermen admire your efforts. Well done!

4 Comments on Selectivity

Nature shortchanged the trout, giving it only a pea-sized brain with which it must deal with intelligent predators such as you and me. Although the trout really isn't very smart, it does hold its own against my fishing friends and me with our fancy degrees. What I don't understand is why volumes of scholarly work should be devoted to catching a creature of such limited intelligence. That's probably a good subject for someone's next book.

The trout does not think; it merely reacts. We fishermen find our sport in trying to tie and fish our flies in such a manner that the trout reacts to them in the same way it does to natural food organisms. This does not require that our flies be scale models of the naturals in order to elicit the desired reaction from the trout. If the trout were smart, it would take every food organism that passes by, but it doesn't. It does take many things that drift by that aren't food and then spits them out. The trout has the ability to recognize an item as food through several previous ingestions of that item. If the item keeps appearing, the trout will become selective to it to the exclusion of all others, even a new bite of real food that is bigger than dozens of the previous item. This must be the most efficient way for the trout to feed, or it would not have evolved with this instinctive behavior. It is this instinctive behavior that we intelligent fishermen confuse with intelligence in the trout.

When a trout feeds selectively on a particular food item, characteristics of any new bite drifting toward the trout must pass muster before the trout will take it. First, it must be moving in the same fashion as the previous bites—dead-drifting, rising to the surface, fluttering on the surface, and so on. If any would-be morsel isn't moving in the manner the

19

trout expects, the trout will not consider it further. Second, trout generally require that some characteristic length of a newly arrived bite match that of the previous ones. This length may be the body length of a nymph or the height of the wings of a mayfly dun, for example. As long as the characteristic length is accurate, the balance of the shape can be approximate, but it must be proportionate. For example, if trout are keying on the height of the wings of a size 18 mayfly, I would not expect an imitation tied with proper wing height and a full-length body on a size 12 hook to be successful. Shape must be preserved but only in a general sense.

I have fished many mayfly hatches where fishermen using Compara-duns, Parachute Duns, and No-Hackle Duns were equally successful, while conventionally hackled duns didn't work at all. The Compara-dun, Parachute, and No-Hackle appear similar only in a very broad sense; perhaps if I viewed them without my glasses, with all of them badly out of focus, they would look alike. To my corrected eye they look very little alike, nor do they look a whole lot like the natural species except at a distance. Yet the trout examined them close up and found all three acceptable. All do ride the water's surface in the same manner. Without question, all imitated characteristics the trout thought were important, which may include attitude on the water and surface impression as well as size and general shape. Trout don't question length-to-diameter ratios of fly bodies, wing width, number of legs on nymphs, and so on, as long as the fly presented to them reasonably incorporates the gross features of the natural without too much exaggeration.

Many of our most successful hatch-matching flies omit much of the detail of the naturals. For example, Comparadun mayflies and No-Hackle Elk Hair Caddis omit legs, which should be clearly visible to the trout. Selective trout in flat water generally prefer these flies to similar imitations that are hackled and thus have some representation of legs (please note that hackle usually serves purposes other than imitation of legs, particularly imitation of the surface impression of insects). If trout demanded detail, flies would not fool them at all. Anything with a hook emanating from its rear end is at best an approximation of the natural organism the fly imitates. Thus, you are satisfying only your desires and not those of the trout if you choose to tie detailed flies. You may end up with less effective flies if you add details of structure that obscure the gross features to which the trout responds. The most effective flies are generally quite simple to tie, but you must give careful thought to what you are imitating.

For example, fishermen frequently match the length of an emerging insect perfectly, only to diminish their efforts by putting tails on the fly—a detail that may mean nothing to the trout. Most floating nymph patterns are tied with tails, yet for sizes smaller than size 16, they work much better without tails. Tails do two things to the floating nymph, both bad. First, they support the rear end of the fly in a horizontal position on the water, while the naturals hang almost vertically with their bodies under the film. The trout prefer what they are used to seeing. The key word here is *seeing*. The body of the floating nymph is more visible to the trout when it is below the meniscus because it is also under the mirror. Trout can see it coming from a greater distance and will move farther to take it. If the imitation is completely on the surface it must pass through the trout's window or the trout will never see it (unless it is a large fly that makes a significant dent in the meniscus). Second, the materials used for tails are much bulkier than the tails of the natural, which are mere filaments. Tails on floating nymphs extend the effective length of the fly and make it difficult for the trout to find the characteristic length it is looking for. On the other hand, many newly emerged duns that do not yet have their wings erect ride the film with their bodies on and parallel to the surface. This stage of the insect's emergence is properly imitated by using a sparse and preferably split tail to assure that the imitation rides the film properly while still preserving the length the trout is looking for. Again, think about what you're imitating as you tie your flies.

Color is sometimes of equal or greater importance than length, but in my experience, only for nymphs such as scuds, Glo-Bugs, and San Juan Worms. When the trout want an orange scud, the length is unimportant. The naturals come in various sizes, and the trout will not look at a scud imitation of any other color, yet they will move several feet to get a nymph that is nothing more than orange fur dubbed onto a hook. Sizes 12 through 18 seem equally effective.

Most of the time color seems unimportant to the success of a small dry fly. I once arrived at the Canyon in early March to find blue-winged olive mayflies hatching, fully a month before I expected them. I didn't have size 18 dry flies in any color but yellow (Parachute Pale Morning Duns left over from the previous season), and the hatching insect was dark gray. The yellow imitation worked so well that I gave several to other fishermen who were frustrated by false rises to conventionally hackled Blue Quills that were a perfect match to the naturals in size and color. The trout knew what they wanted, but color wasn't on their list. If you have the right dry fly pattern in the right size but the wrong color, you should ignore the color. The trout probably will, too. Still, I want color on my side if possible. If that is not possible, I try to fish light or dark flies to imitate light or dark insects, respectively. Usually even that is unnecessary, as my example indicates.

I have encountered a few dry-fly situations in which color did seem important to the trout. All of those few occasions involved imitations of large insects. Trout generally seem more particular about imitations of large insects. Perhaps those occasions were manifestations of that particularity, or perhaps they were coincidental. I don't know.

In most obvious dry-fly situations in which trout are rising regularly, the trout will be selective in their feeding. The most important thing to do first is to find out what is on the water so that you can match it. Usually this requires little more than dipping an insect off the water's surface with an aquarium net and watching the rise form to determine which stage of the insect the trout is taking.

There are several characteristics of the rise form that will help you determine upon which stage of the insect's life cycle the trout are feeding. If you can't see what a trout is taking, but the rise is slow and deliberate, with the tail of the trout visible as the trout completes the rise, the trout is taking something flush in the film such as a spinner or emerger. If you can't find spinners on the water, choose an emerger. If you see the trout's nose above the water, or there is a bubble left on the surface after the rise, it is taking adults. If you can't see the adults on the water, the trout is probably taking midges. If the rise is splashy, the trout is taking either a large insect (which you should be able to see) or one that is moving, such as an emerging caddis or fluttering mayfly dun. Try twitching your fly a bit. Finally, if none of the trout or only its dorsal fin is visible as it rises, the trout is taking the emerging insect while it is still below the film. Fish the nymphal imitation of the hatching insect (nymph, floating nymph, caddis pupa, midge pupa). There will be times when there are two or more insects hatching, and what the trout is taking isn't obvious. Such times make dedicated hatch-matchers compulsive to get back to the Platte to solve the puzzle. What I should have done always becomes clear to me as I am driving home.

5 Trout Food

It would be nice if everything trout eat had a well-defined size so that you could match it precisely. For that matter, it would also be nice if all size 16 hooks were the same size, but they aren't. When I refer to hook sizes, I mean Tiemco TMC 100 hooks unless I specify otherwise. These are slightly longer of shank than the corresponding Mustad 94840, which is the most common reference but is of very poor quality in the smaller sizes necessary to imitate most South Platte insects.

The sizes of insects are more problematical than those of hooks. The size of a given insect may change over the course of the hatching of that insect. A particular mayfly may be size 22 in June, size 26 in August, and size 24 in both July and October. When you prepare for a given hatch, tie one or two of each pattern in a size larger and a size smaller than the size I indicate. If you don't need them for that particular hatch, they will work for something else.

Fred Arbona offers a very good discussion of the size variations of mayflies in his excellent book, *Mayflies, the Angler and the Trout.* He explains that the mayfly must maintain a certain moisture content in order to shed its skin and become a spinner that can mate. As the season becomes warmer and the sun more intense, the insect decreases in size so that it absorbs less of the drying sunshine. Imitations that worked in mid-June may be too large by early July. Some insects may also confine their hatching to cloudy days. As an added complication, a given hatch may be composed of several closely related species that look alike but are of different sizes.

Perhaps the adaptation of the various insect species to sun intensity also plays a role in determining the color of the insects. Early- and late-season mayflies are usually quite dark. The one dark summertime mayfly hatches at night and in the early-morning hours, then molts and mates before the sun is intense. Its largest surface area—its wings—are white. The early- and late-season caddisflies and midges on the Platte are dark, too. As a rule, you will encounter light-colored insects on the Platte only during a six-week period, sometime from mid-June through July. This may explain why many of our most popular dry-fly patterns are dark. I'll let you decide how to classify a white-winged black mayfly that hatches for four months, beginning in late June.

I have organized this discussion of trout foods of the South Platte in the following way: I first identify the family of organism (mayfly, midge, etc.). Next, I give the place (Cheesman Canyon or Spinney), and then individual species, presented in the sequence of their emergence at that place. With this organization, I can discuss the better hatches at each place and then note only the differences to be found when you fish the same hatch at the other section of the river. You don't need a thorough discussion of Blue-Winged Olives for Cheesman Canyon, followed by a thorough discussion of Blue-Winged Olives for Spinney Mountain Ranch. They are the same critter, and you imitate and fish the hatch the same way at both places; all that's different is where and when. This organization does put the onus on you to pay attention to your location as you read this chapter. If you have the concentration to tie a blood-knot, that shouldn't strain you.

MAYFLIES

Spinney Mountain Ranch

Pale Morning Duns

There are two super hatches that keep the fisherman occupied from about the second week of June through mid-November. The first, the pale morning dun (PMD), is short lived but offers the most exciting fishing of the year. The PMD hatches typically begin about 10:00 A.M. and last until 1:00 P.M. The trout immediately begin feeding upon them, but if the hatch is not a heavy one you may not see even a single dun, for the trout seem to get every emerger. Trout move considerable distances to get the nymphs as they rise to the surface and take them with a splashy rise that you may confuse with the rise to an emerging caddis. A small tan caddis emerges at the same time, and any given fish may be taking either. The caddis hatch in greater numbers in riffles, so if trout in the riffles aren't taking your mayfly emerger, try a size 18 Elk Hair Caddis or Devil Bug. The habitat for the PMD is the riffles and water with current sufficiently fast to keep silt washed from the bottom.

The PMD may fool you unless you know the trick. The first time I fished this hatch here was the year the Spinney section opened. I had just returned from fishing Montana spring creeks, my head swelled by my success at imitating the PMDs there. When the PMDs started to emerge I seined a dun from the surface, put it in my flybox for accurate size comparison, and confidently selected a size 16 emerger. An hour later I had had probably fifty false rises and had not hooked one trout! Time to look at the water again; but there was nothing else on the water. By some good fortune, I seined a yellow blob from the surface just as the dun was beginning to emerge from its shuck. When I laid the shuck beside the newly emerged dun the problem was obvious. The shuck was considerably shorter than the body of the dun that emerged from it! I had been getting false rises to a size 16 emerger; I was suddenly catching every trout I cast to after switching to the size 18 emerger. Now you know the trick. The PMD is telescopic in its mechanical structure. The nymph is size 18, while the dun is size 16, or even 14. This telescopic structure probably occurs with other mayflies. If you are getting false rises, something about the pattern appeals to the trout. Try the same pattern in a size smaller before you change to a completely different pattern.

Dun imitations are very effective at the end of the hatch when only an occasional dun can be seen. Fish a size 16 Comparadun along the banks just after the hatch has ended and you are certain to pick up several fish before the trout stop looking up to feed. The best fish I have caught at Spinney, a twenty-two-inch brown of about three and one-half pounds, was taken in exactly this manner.

The spinnerfall for the PMD may occur at night, for I have not observed late afternoon spinner flights here as I have on Montana spring creeks. There is a large olive spinner (#14-16) on the water in the early morning that may be the PMD spinner, but I have never seen it in sufficient numbers to bring the fish up.

Fish a size 18 Pheasant Tail Nymph year-round at Spinney and particularly during May through July. It is a very high confidence imitation of the PMD nymph.

Tricos

The second super hatch in the Spinney area is the small white-winged black mayfly, which we all know and love as the Trico. This hatch displays the entire life cycle of the mayfly over a very short time and provides the opportunity to be satiated with catching trout every time you fish it. I tie 90 percent of my imitations for this hatch on size 24 hooks. Size 24 is usually as small as I have to use for body length in order to get a good imitation of the natural. During August, the natural insect has a body length smaller than size 24 and you may find a size 26 necessary; at other times, the females are as large as size 22. I tie all my winged imitations with the wings almost twice the body length, then trim to the proper length on stream with the imitation sitting beside a natural.

The Trico hatch may begin as early as mid-June and thus overlap the PMD hatch. On several occasions I have been frustrated by the inability to catch trout that I thought were rising to PMD emergers. When I finally stopped casting to find out what was going on, I found Trico spinners on the water, which the trout preferred to the much larger PMDs that were still hatching. During the summer months, the female Tricos (olive abdomen, black thorax) begin hatching about one hour after dawn. Trout take floating nymphs and/or emerger patterns for perhaps one and one-half hours. Seldom will you see a fish taking the newly emerged duns. The hatch is not too dense, but a good fisherman may catch a half-dozen fish while it is on.

Spinner clouds will form toward the end of the hatch (9:00 A.M.), and the fish will switch to spinners as soon as they hit the water, even though duns will still be hatching. The switch is subtle. As soon as you see the tails of rising trout, switch to a spinner pattern. Seine a natural from the water and trim the wing length of the imitation to match it. The female spinners are a little larger than the male and have a different colored abdomen. They fall thirty minutes to one hour after the males. Some fishermen carry spinners with olive abdomens. I have yet to encounter a trout feeding on spinners here that wouldn't take an all-black spinner.

The male Tricos begin to hatch at dusk. The air is cooler at this hour, and with no direct sun the duns must ride the current for a longer period to dry their wings. The trout will take duns in the evening that they wouldn't take in the morning. Comparaduns, Parachute Duns, floating nymphs, and emergers will all work for as long as you care to fish into the dark.

Later in the season (about October), the nights become too cold for the Tricos to hatch at night. The two daily hatches become one, beginning at about 9:00 A.M. and lasting about three hours. The hatch may be quite dense, and duns ride the water longer. During the late season, the trout switch to duns in preference to emergers. The Comparadun is usually the fly of choice, although, for reasons of their own, the trout sometimes prefer a size 20-22 Adams. Spinners will invariably be on the water while the duns are hatching. If you don't see duns disappearing or if you see the trout's tail as it rises it is probably taking spinners. Typically the action will last till noon.

Fishing with the duns or emergers requires no special tricks. One small piece of knowledge can help you increase your catch on spinners. When the spinners are on the water, the trout hold just below the surface and cruise back and forth taking four or five spinners before they go back down. By cruising side to side, they increase their food intake for the effort to remain in the stronger currents at the surface of the stream. When they encounter a spinner it will be only inches from their nose, and they must make an instantaneous decision whether to take. If it's the right size, they probably will take it. You can take advantage of this behavior very easily. First, from a position downstream of the trout, crawl on your hands and knees to within fifteen feet of the trout, and get as comfortable as you can to fish from your knees. Cast to the side and adjust the line length until your spinner is no more than six inches in front of the trout's average position. Place your fly in front of the place you hope the trout will be. When the fly has drifted to no more than six inches behind the trout, pick up the fly and, without false casting, put it six inches in front of the trout again. Continue until he takes, then set the hook very quickly (but gently). When you are fishing one-foot drifts, you will probably make a dozen or more casts in a minute.

The point of this technique is that the trout cannot see a spinner coming when it is three feet away; the trout's window when it is just below the surface is too small. You are wasting time if you place your spinner three feet in front of the trout and watch as it drifts five feet or more, knowing that if it is as little as a few inches to the side of the trout, the fish will never see it. You will catch more fish with many short drifts of spinners placed just beyond the end of the trout's nose. (You should also note that this is true only for situations when the trout is holding just below the surface; when the trout is holding a foot or more deep, your fly should be placed several feet forward of the trout's position.)

Nymph fishing during the hours when nothing is happening on the surface can be quite good using a fat size 24 nymph of either peacock herl or medium olive-brown dubbing. The nymph should be about half as thick as it is long to match the proportions of the natural insect and should be dead-drifted along the bottom.

Other Mayflies

There are blue-winged olive mayflies (BWO) in the Spinney Mountain Ranch section of the Platte, but I have never encountered a dense hatch there. The trout will take a floating nymph or emerger in a size 18 or 20 during the fall, and you do see a few duns on the water in October at about noon. Where there is a fall BWO hatch, there should be a spring BWO hatch, but I have never encountered a fishable hatch. There are also speckled spinners in about size 16 over the water in late June and early July, but I have never observed trout feeding on them.

Cheesman Canyon

Blue-Winged Olives

The premier mayfly hatch for Cheesman Canyon is the BWO hatch that occurs in the spring and fall. If you awaken one morning in early May to find the weather warm and cloudy, quit your job if necessary, but be in the Canyon by 11:00 A.M. If it is a good BWO day you will endure drizzle or snow by mid-afternoon. You will also find trout rising to a hatch that offers several duns per square foot along the drift lanes. The trout become incredibly selective during these dense hatches and often will not even come up to look at a dun imitation. Your dun imitation has so much competition from naturals that it would be sheer luck if the trout chose it anyway. Even so, the trout take a size 20 floating nymph with so much confidence that you feel guilty every time you set the hook, which may add up to a real guilt trip. There are sometimes two different flies on the water, one about an 18 and the other a 20 or 22. The size 20 floating nymph seems to work for both. The emerger pattern will sometimes outfish the floating nymph. Carry both of them.

During less dense hatches the trout will also feed on duns. A size 18-22 Comparadun works quite well, as do Parachute Duns if you prefer that pattern. There always seem to be some trout that become selective to fluttering duns, and for such fish conventionally hackled BWOs, Blue Quills, or Blue Duns work well. A splashy rise usually indicates such a preference. You may find that giving your fly a slight twitch about one foot in front of the trout will help. There are times when a fly two sizes too large (#14-16) works better for trout that prefer fluttering duns. I find such behavior in trout disappointing and offensive. Oh, well.

Toward the end of the BWO hatch you may notice that you haven't caught a fish for quite a while, even though BWOs are obviously still hatching. There are two probable reasons for this. First, BWO spinners may be coming back to the water for oviposition, and the trout may have switched to the spinner if there were enough of them. A size 18-20 Rusty Spinner works just fine. Second, a tiny midge may have started to hatch at about that time; a size 26 Griffiths Gnat usually solves this problem.

The fall BWO hatch in the Canyon provides a very pleasant change from the mobs fishing the Tricos at Spinney. As an added bonus, there may be some Trico activity in the Canyon at this time as well. High summertime waterflows seem to delay the Trico activity in the Canyon, and in high water years you may find BWOs and Tricos hatching together, simultaneously with Trico spinners falling. I've encountered this situation several times. Fortunately, the trout wanted only floating nymphs and ignored the spinners. (Sometimes the fish gods keep things joyously simple, but only for the pure of heart.)

You should plan to be in the Canyon by 10:00 A.M. in the spring and fall. The BWO nymphs are swimmers that become quite active at about this time prior to their daily hatch. The trout think a size 18 gray RS-2 looks more like food than the real thing. You'll have two hours of great nymph fishing before you see the first rise.

Pale Morning Duns

PMDs usually hatch in the Canyon during July. PMDs come in two species, big and little. The big one occurs at Spinney, and the little one is found in the Canyon. The PMD in the Canyon is about size 18, although a size 20 fly sometimes fishes better later in the season. The turbulent waters of the Canyon do not have the strength of surface tension that the flatter waters at Spinney possess, and as a consequence the individual flies are able to hatch in less time. There is more food available on the surface in duns drying their wings than there is below the surface in emergers trying to penetrate the meniscus. What this means to the fisherman is that a Comparadun works about as well as or even better than the emerger in the turbulent areas where the PMD hatches are best. Again, I have not observed PMD spinner falls here, although I know they occur.

One of my favorite nymphs for summer fishing in the Canyon is the Pheasant Tail Nymph in about size 18. It is a perfect match for the dark brown nymph of the PMD. It seems to work all day long in the riffles and pockets of the Canyon, which, not coincidentally, is the habitat of the PMD nymph.

Tricos

Trico activity in the Canyon is usually best in August through mid-September. The spinner fall is usually of shorter duration in the Canyon than at Spinney, but it is still quite good. Everything discussed in the Spinney section applies here, too.

Other Mayflies

Cheesman Canyon must have as many species of insects as any western river. On several occasions I've encountered good hatches of mayflies that I hadn't seen before and haven't seen since. One I have seen several times in September is a giant yellow mayfly, perhaps a size 10, which looks like a huge PMD. It creates a real commotion trying to get off the water, and trout really nail it when they see it. I have seen perhaps a dozen of these insects in the past ten years. You will probably have similar experiences with flies you encounter and are prepared for the next time, but next time the hatch just doesn't occur. The hatches discussed above, however, are reliable.

MIDGES

For the purposes of the fisherman on the South Platte, there are three species of midge: the little midge, the big midge, and the green midge. "The green midge" is actually an abbreviation of the name for a small green winged insect whose complete name is "*The goddamned-spinneymountaingreenringtailedsonofabitch midge.*" I'm not making this up; all the really good fishermen there call it that so I must assume that to be its real name. More about it later.

The little midges and the green midge hatches offer the ultimate challenge in fly fishing. The first lesson the trout have taught me about midge fishing is that your fly must drift right over the trout. A foot to either side just isn't good enough. The difficulty arises because most of the time a trout will not move even a few inches from the drift lane it is holding in to take a midge *from the surface.* As a consequence, you may have on exactly the right fly but still not take a trout because your presentation was not accurate enough. Part of this difficulty arises from the same optical phenomenon discussed for fishing Trico spinners. I once crawled up behind the rock dam at the tail of the Icebox pool in the Canyon to fish to a trout rising to midges about ten feet in front of me, where I could see its every movement. I fished to that trout for about an hour before I gave up, but I still learned a lot about midge fishing from the experience. The wind was blowing and only twice in that hour did I suceed in floating my #26 Griffiths Gnat directly over the trout. The trout took it both times and both times I set the hook too quickly.

I did notice that the trout would move a foot or so to take things I couldn't see, presumably pupae under the surface. Only when an adult went directly over the trout did it take an adult from the surface. Trout holding two feet deep have a window that is several feet in diameter, and they may rise from that depth through even fast currents to take a large insect. They usually will not do so to take a tiny insect. The calories gained do not balance those expended in the effort. I finally realized that trout rising to midges generally do so in very flat, quiet water and hold just below the surface. This one was holding in water only a few inches deep. Its window could have been no larger than several inches in diameter. Tiny midge adults will not indent the meniscus, and, unless an adult passes through the trout's window, the trout will never detect it. On the other hand, pupae under the surface are also under the mirror where the trout can see them, and the trout will move a greater distance to take a pupa simply because the trout knows it's there.

This optical phenomenon partially explains the trout's general preference for emergers rather than adult insects. The emerging insects are still under the mirror where they are visible to the trout, while most of the adults are blocked from the trout's view by the mirror over its world. I felt a little better when I realized not only that I had to overcome wind and my own frailties, but also that the ghosts of physicists past—Snell, Faraday, and Maxwell—were all on the side of that trout. I was probably the 817th fisherman to figure out the problem that year, but I still had done so all by myself. I now switch to a pupa and tiny split shot at the slightest snub of a dry midge imitation.

The second lesson the trout have taught me about midge fishing is that you must have flies that are tiny! You must carry midge imitations in sizes 26 and 28 if you are to be prepared for most of the midge hatches on the South Platte. Even with flies that match the naturals in size and a good hatch, I never experience the success fishing midge hatches that I enjoy during the hatches of mayflies and caddisflies. The problem is not one of pattern, but one of accuracy of presentation and size of the imitation. Successful fishing of a good midge hatch is not measured in dozens of trout released; if you hook three or four you've done quite well.

Cheesman Canyon

The Little Midges

The little midges in the Canyon range from size 20 to size 46, with the latter size being the most common. All kidding aside, it is not unusual to encounter trout rising to a hatch of midges that are simply too small to imitate even with size 28s. Don't let this discourage you because there are midge hatches almost every day of the year that can be imitated. The little midges provide some of the most difficult fishing to be found, but if you succeed, nothing else in fly fishing is as satisfying.

Any time you encounter trout rising to a hatch of small midges the first fly to try is a Griffiths Gnat. I generally try one tied on a size 26 Partridge Marinaro Midge hook, regardless of the size insect on the water.

That fly in that size is the most reliable imitation for small midges on the South Platte that I have found. That particular hook is shorter than the Tiemco 26 and has a wide gape. It is no more difficult to handle than any other small fly, but because of the small mass of the fly, you should fish it with 7X tippet in order to get a natural drift. Some authors recommend that you clip the hackle from under the fly if the trout are fussy. This has worked for me on a few occasions, but usually the fact that the trout won't take the hackled fly means that they want something under the mirror where they can see it.

The second fly of choice is a pupa imitation. Seine an adult from the surface and choose either a Quill Midge or Muskrat Nymph the same length as or very slightly longer than the adult. If you're having difficulty fishing a tiny fly you can't see, try the following: Tie on a size 20 Adams with 6X tippet. Then tie a sixteen-inch section of 7X tippet to the eye of the Adams. Next, take another section of tippet (say 5X) and tie a double surgeon's knot about eight inches from the end of the 7X tippet and trim both ends of the 5X at the knot. Tie the pupa to the end of the 7X tippet and crimp a tiny split shot above the surgeon's knot. The Adams is a strike indicator. If it goes under or there is a nearby rise, gently set the hook. You may be lucky enough to find a trout that prefers the Adams to what it had been eating. Be very careful as you release it or it may set that second hook in your hide. I once dropped a trout as I was trying to remove the Adams and the second hook caught in my hand. I wanted either the Adams out of the trout's mouth or the pupa out of my hand, and I didn't care which, as long as it was quick!

Some fish will become selective to emerging midges that are half in and half out of their shuck. The key in this case is that the total length of the fly should be about twice the length of the adult. Choose the appropriate-size stillborn midge pattern and trim the shuck to the proper length to achieve this total length. I am convinced that the conventional midge pattern with a sparse tail also represents a stillborn insect. It often works when nothing else will. I suspect that its surface impression accurately imitates that of the emerging midge.

If you're sure you have fished the proper size imitations but nothing has worked, the trout have probably become selective to motion. Perhaps the rise to the surface or the wiggling required for the insect to break the meniscus and emerge from the shuck provides the stimulus that causes the trout to take the insect. Dick Walker, a British author, has observed that emerging midges in an aquarium swim away when he puts his hand into the water. If emerging stream midges sense the presence of trout and flee, the splashy rises you sometimes observe from trout feeding on midges make more sense. In any event, motion of the fly is sometimes the key to success during a midge hatch. Fortunately, the trout don't require a wiggling fly; linear motion is good enough. With whatever fly you have on, try dragging it about six inches across the surface when it is about two feet in front of the trout. This may serve only to disturb the meniscus and focus the trout's attention on your fly, but it's worked for me.

If you still can't catch the risers, you may have to console yourself by catching fish on nymphs. Put on an appropriately sized Muskrat Nymph, Quill Midge, or Brassie and enough weight to get the nymph to the bottom quickly. Cast about twenty feet straight upstream in water two to four feet deep, keeping your rod tip up after the cast. Strip line in as the nymph sinks while still keeping the rod tip up. When you think it is near the bottom, slowly push your rod tip straight up until the tip of your flyline has dragged a distance of one to one and a half feet. Slowly count to three, then repeat. Quite often the first lift will have induced a trout to take the nymph and the second lift will set the hook. This works especially well during spring midge hatches. If it doesn't work, try a dead drift before you change nymphs.

Crane Flies

One phenomenon you may observe in Cheesman Canyon during May is unnerving. A big fish may jump completely out of the water five or six times during a period of a few seconds, seemingly gone berserk. When a fish does this it is likely to be chasing a relative of the small midges, the crane fly. These insects are large, about one and one-half inches long, and they flutter across the water in a manner reminiscent of a daddy longlegs spider. I have not fished this hatch successfully, but from what I read, a Hewitt Skater should be the fly that mimics the crane fly behavior. The great men of our sport suggest fishing it down and across, with short strips like a streamer (fished dry). I've been planning to try this, and I hope this will be the year I do. You will encounter trout chasing adult crane flies so seldom, however, that you probably won't miss five fish per season if you aren't prepared for them, as I never am.

Spinney Mountain

The Little Midges

The little midges at Spinney Mountain behave just like the little midges in the Canyon, and there are a lot of them. May and June have particularly good hatches; fish the deeper runs with a Quill Midge or Brassie for exciting nymphing. The slow, flat water will make you be at your very best to succeed with dries. Nothing here is intrinsically different from conditions at the Canyon.

The Big Midge

The big midge at Spinney was designed with fly fishing in mind. This insect is about one inch long and rides the water a long time as it hatches. A Fore-and-Aft or Renegade in size 18 imitates the adult quite well, even though the artificial is smaller than the natural insect. Full-size imitations do not work as well; I suspect the indentation of the meniscus by the feet of the natural is more closely matched by the size 18 Fore-and-Aft. The trout are always on the alert for these insects, so during periods when nothing is hatching, put on either fly and fish it anywhere. I particularly like the outsides of deep bends, right against the banks. Don't be too quick to set the hook, for the trout take it slowly and confidently.

The big midges hatch in the early morning (7:00–9:00 A.M.) during June through mid-July. They appear to be the same insect as the one that hatches in profusion on the reservoir at about the same time. I have encountered hatches in two different types of habitat. The slow bends with silty bottoms have excellent hatches of the big black midge. Areas at the foot of riffles have good hatches of a large green midge that may be the female of the species; it is the same size as the black one. The trout prefer the emerger to the adult. I have had good luck in these areas fishing a fly I tied as a caddis pupa, a bright green antron soft-hackle in size 16, fished on the surface but not greased. This is one dry-fly situation in which color seems important.

The Green Midge

The green midge has a bright green body with white wings. It hatches in the mornings in June and July, typically right before the PMD hatch or just after the Trico hatch (but before the spinner fall). It is one of the reasons I love fly fishing, because it presents a puzzle I haven't solved. I have one flybox that contains nothing but various green midge imitations in sizes 22–24. Every time I fish the green midge hatch I have a complete new series of imitations, one of which will invariably take one or two fish but from that day on will be useless. A green-bodied Griffiths Gnat sometimes works, and occasionally that same fly with the hackle clipped underneath works even better—but not consistently. A peacock-bodied Griffiths Gnat works just as well. Some fishermen swear by a small green Fore-and-Aft, but it has been only an average producer for me. An olive biot-bodied No-Name Midge has its moments, but is on average only slightly more effective than a peacock-bodied Griffiths Gnat.

I have seen only one fisherman fish the green midge hatch with true success. I was fishing flat water when the midges started to hatch, and the trout started to rise to them immediately. I was on about my third pattern change when a fisherman about fifty yards upstream asked me what the fish were taking. I answered, "A size 22 green midge, but I've never found anything that works very well," and resumed my fly changing. He was little more than a beginner and was doing a lot of things wrong. He fumbled for five minutes to tie on a fly and immediately caught an eight-inch rainbow. Small trout will bite anything once, so I thought nothing of it. He continued casting to the middle of the river, not to any particular trout. Fifteen minutes later he released his sixth good fish and I could stand no more. I asked if he would mind showing me his fly, and of course he was pleased to do so. It was the first midge imitation he had tried to tie, a size 22. The pattern is properly called a No-Name Midge, although neither Schwiebert nor Shenk would claim this fly. He had used two turns of cheap, oversized grizzly hackle and a body dubbed with enough dark gray muskrat fur to make a size 22 fur coat. The first little trout had shredded the body so that the fly now had a scraggly tail of muskrat fur about one-half inch long. The trout were obviously taking the fly as a stillborn. I had been fishing a beautifully tied size 22 green stillborn without success. I was so disgusted that I went to the riffles and fished a Royal Wulff for the rest of the morning. I couldn't bring myself to try to imitate the other man's fly, but you may be amused by my stillborn midge pattern.

I will erect a bronze plaque on the banks of the Platte to honor the fisherman who shows me the *green* fly that consistently takes fish on the surface during the green midge hatch. I insist that it be green. My childlike faith will not allow me to believe that the trout would actually prefer a fly that is obviously the wrong color, all evidence to the contrary notwithstanding.

I have had great success nymphing with the Green Machine, the pupal imitation for the green midge. It also works when the trout key on the emerging pupa in the film. Fish it with the smallest split shot to get it under the surface. The mating behavior of the green midges is the easiest part of that insect's life cycle to imitate. When you see them on the water joined at the tail, put on a size 20 green-bodied Fore-and-Aft. It's so easy you'll think you're a genius. Mating occurs on flat water and is not difficult to spot if you watch for it. I have seen it most often in mid-afternoon.

CADDISFLIES

Caddisflies present few problems to the South Platte angler, perhaps because there are so few of them. I spent several years being apprehensive about them based on all I had read of the difficulties in coping with them. The South Platte, however, does not offer the prolific caddis hatches found on freestone rivers. The hatches are sparse and the trout are not difficult to fool. The greatest difficulty you will encounter is in recognizing that a caddis hatch is in progress. Usually, your only clue will be a few splashy rises or the sight of an occasional fish jumping. Furthermore, you could do 99 percent of your caddis imitating with only three flies, all size 18: the Elk Hair Caddis (preferably without hackle), the Devil Bug, and a dark soft-hackle nymph.

Cheesman Canyon

Caddis hatches begin in the Canyon in mid-May. These early hatches occur mid-afternoon. I have not observed trout surface feeding on these early caddisflies. You may spot an occasional adult wiggling on the surface. It will be dark, about size 18. A dark Hare's Ear soft hackle fished through deep holes and runs dead-drifted or with a slow lift of the nymph from the bottom at the end of the dead drift are the most effective ways to fish this hatch. The soft-hackled fly will be only one of several flies you should be trying during afternoons in May in the Canyon. The hatch is very localized. You may find one while your partner twenty-five yards away does not. The hatch will be short lived, and it is very likely that you will miss it if you have found something else the trout want. In all probability, something else will be working better during such afternoons. In particular, Brassies, RS-2s, orange scuds, and tan scuds are usually quite effective at this time of the year.

During June and July, caddis hatches switch to the early evening, with the greatest activity at dusk. Fish to rising trout with either an Elk Hair Caddis or a Devil Bug. Size 16 and 18 both work. I prefer a dark fly, although there is so little light that I'm not convinced it matters. Don't overlook caddis as a searching fly during the summer months. Fish the same size 18 Elk Hair along the banks and particularly in the quiet eddies near big rocks from dawn until about 11:00 A.M. You'll be surprised at how many fish in quiet waters are looking up and are willing to take a caddis.

August isn't a particularly good month for fishing the Canyon with anything other than Trico imitations. I haven't encountered caddis hatches during that month. A size 18-20 Elk Hair Caddis can provide exciting fishing during September. Fish all the shallow pockets, quiet eddies near big rocks, and riffles. I was fishing a nymph during a September afternoon several years ago when I noticed several splashy rises ten yards downstream. I was ready to change nymphs anyway and on a hunch tied a size 18 Hare's Ear soft-hackle to the end of the 6X tippet I had been using. A few minutes later I spotted the biggest trout I had ever seen, just upstream. It had come out from an undercut rock to feed on the hatching caddis. I cast the soft-hackle well upstream, and it was two feet deep when it reached the trout. When I thought the nymph had time to be behind the trout I gently tightened and, with my heart in my throat, discovered that the trout was solidly hooked. Ten minutes later, two fishermen with cameras happened by and stopped to watch. I am still grateful because I now have pictures of a twenty-six-inch hen rainbow, estimated to weigh about eight pounds, the largest trout I've ever caught. I still have that soft-hackled Hare's Ear and look at it every time I get ready to tie more of them. The dead-drifted soft-hackle has worked for me in many caddis hatches since.

Spinney Mountain

The caddis hatches at Spinney Mountain are similar in time and size to those of Cheesman Canyon. The May hatches also occur in mid-afternoon. The June and July hatches are considerably better than those in the Canyon, and some even occur at civilized times. A size 18 yellow or tan caddis hatches at about 10:00 A.M. during mid-June through July, often during the PMD hatch. It is an especially good hatch in riffle areas where the trout will move a considerable distance to get an Elk Hair Caddis or Devil Bug. Cast quartering downstream, allow it to dead-drift several feet, and follow with a very slight twitch. The twitch is often the stimulus that causes the trout to rise to it. In flat-water areas down-stream from riffles a dark Devil Bug seems to work all afternoon, bring-ing trout to the surface at times when it is apparent that no hatch is in progress. It represents an emerging or stillborn caddis, which the trout must see enough of to remain on the lookout. I fish it and an Elk Hair Caddis as attractors in flat water (particularly along cut banks) where conventional attractors such as a Royal Wulff usually aren't too effec-tive. Mid-summer also offers hatches and ovipositing caddis at dusk with naturals as large as size 14. Try all three of the caddis patterns, including the soft-hackle, on the surface either dead-drifted or with an occasional twitch. Remember that the male Tricos and small midges will also be hatching at dusk during the mid-summer months, but typically not pro-fusely in the riffles where the caddis are more prevalent. If you are fish-ing a slow-water area unsuccessfully it may be because the trout are on either the Tricos or the midges.

There is a yellow microcaddis that hatches in late afternoon through most of the summer. I've seen it most often at about 3:00 P.M., often simultaneously with a small midge. The caddis is about size 26 and rides the film for an extended distance after hatching, wiggling for all it's worth. A size 26 Elk Hair Caddis may take an occasional trout. When I conclude that the trout are on the microcaddis, I pause to reflect that among the principals of this contest, I am the intelligent one, the one able to analyze the situation, review the options, and select the optimal response. I then go look for a new spot, one that offers green chile and Dos Equis. This usually requires that you pack your gear and leave, but if you want to cope with a really difficult hatch you must be prepared to pay the price. Fifteen dollars (for the meal and beer) does not seem an excessive price to pay to halt the assault on my ego.

STONEFLIES

Stoneflies do not provide the South Platte angler with the dramatic dry-fly fishing that those insects offer on freestone rivers. There are hatches of large golden stoneflies, but I have never seen a trout take an adult from the surface. However, the fact that the hatch occurs does create some excellent dry-fly fishing in Cheesman Canyon. The large golden stoneflies hatch in Cheesman Canyon during June. These insects hatch in an unusual fashion: The nymph crawls out of the water, usually onto a streamside rock, where the shuck splits and the adult crawls from the nymphal shuck. After mating, the adult females return to the water for oviposition. It is at this time that the trout take adult stoneflies. I have never seen an adult golden stonefly in Cheesman Canyon; I've seen only the freshly hatched shucks. I believe that the females return to the water at night—which is the most reasonable explanation for the success of a size 10-12 Rio Grande King Trude, the only large dry fly I have found that takes trout in the Canyon. It works early in the morning, from dawn until 10:00 A.M. during June, precisely the time when the stonefly shucks begin appearing on the rocks. The fact that it is black bodied is not inconsistent with it being a golden stonefly imitation if, in fact, the adults are on the water at night when color is probably not discernible to the trout.

There are also small golden stoneflies in Cheesman Canyon in significant numbers. I believe that the nymphs of the small golden stone are the reason that small tan mayfly nymphs (RS-2, about size 16) work well for much of the summer. The hatch itself is somewhat unpredictable. I have encountered it only during late summer and early fall. The small golden stoneflies hatch in the surface film, like mayflies. If you have a few yellow Elk Hair Caddis imitations and a tan nymph in sizes 16-18 you'll be as well prepared to fish this hatch as I am.

During the spring BWO hatches you may encounter tiny early brown stoneflies (about size 20) also hatching in the surface film in a manner similar to mayflies. A tiny, dark No-Hackle Caddis may take an occasional trout. I have seen a larger dark stonefly (about size 12-14) at this time that also appears to hatch in the film, and trout take them with a splashy rise. I have seen so few of them that I haven't tried to imitate them as trout have been steadily rising to BWOs and midges every time I have seen them.

There are reasonable numbers of adult golden stoneflies in some riffle areas of the Spinney section of the Platte during June through early July, coincident with the PMD hatch. Again, I have never seen a trout take one, so I don't bother carrying imitations of them. There are usually caddis hatching in the riffles when the adult stoneflies are present, and as I'm usually catching fish on an Elk Hair Caddis, I don't know whether I'm missing a lot of fun or not. If you discover that what the trout really want is a size 10-12 golden stone adult, please let me know. There are also a few small golden stoneflies (size 16-18) hatching in the film at about this same time, and the small caddis imitation I'm usually fishing should imitate these as well.

SCUDS

Scuds are something of a mystery to me. Most of the scuds you find by seining in Cheesman Canyon are olive-gray; most of the scud imitations that catch a lot of trout there are tan or orange. I carry and fish Olive-Gray Scuds, but seldom have the success with them that the other colors provide. The Olive-Gray Scud does work early in the morning in Cheesman Canyon during the summer months. It can be fished either dead-drifted or with short strips. The crustacean it imitates is a relatively good swimmer, which darts about in short bursts. The reason for fishing scuds in the early morning is that they exhibit behavioral drift. They let go of their connections to the bottom and freely drift, thus distributing themselves throughout the stream. This activity occurs at night, and after eating them at night, the trout continue to watch for them during the morning hours.

When the other two colors of scud work, there is nothing indifferent about the trout's reaction to them. The trout will often move several feet to get a Tan or Orange Scud, and you will experience periods when you can hook a trout every few minutes. It's almost as if you're fishing a hatch you have matched exactly.

The Tan Scud starts to work in March in both the Spinney Mountain and Cheesman Canyon sections of the Platte. I have found scuds in the Spinney section in particular that are tan. Scuds come in two varieties, big and little. The tan ones I have found by seining have always been small, about size 16 (TMC 2487 hook). Larger imitations (#12, TMC 2487 hook), however, do work. I was recently informed by another reliable fisherman that he has found large tan scuds at Spinney.

The most exciting nymph fishing you will ever encounter occurs in Cheesman Canyon during May and early June. The trout will take anything orange that even remotely resembles a scud! The action starts at about 10:00 A.M. and lasts for several hours. The trout move so far to get an Orange Scud that it is not unusual to see your strike indicators move a foot upstream after a trout takes the nymph and returns to its holding position. If you've been having difficulty with nymphing, this is the time to be on stream. You will quickly learn what a strike looks like because you will have so many of them. Just be certain that you are using enough weight to get the nymph on the bottom. The trout will do their part.

I have never found an orange scud in a seine sample on any river anywhere. I have seen a number of them in my aquarium, however, and they were all dead. The life cycle of the scud is apparently such that they die in the spring. After death they turn a dirty orange-tan, which is not too different in color from boiled shrimp but with a lighter hue. A dead scud cannot cling to the bottom and thus is available to the trout. A scud is a substantial bite, and judging by the trout's relish for them, the fish must see a lot of them.

The effectiveness of the Tan Scud in Cheesman Canyon is puzzling. There are so few tan scuds in my seine samples that I am convinced that the trout must see more of the olive-gray scuds than tan ones. One possible explanation given by several authors is that the periodic molting of the shell to allow for growth leaves the scud with a new soft shell that is light in color but which slowly darkens as it hardens. The trout apparently prefer the softer-shelled crustaceans to their darker brethren, although this explanation is not satisfying to me. I certainly can't refute it, but it seems to me that wild creatures do not survive by being finicky eaters.

That trout would turn down olive-gray scuds awaiting a freshly molted one just doesn't square with my observations of trout behavior. Still, I know that I have fished Olive-Gray Scuds to visible trout that wouldn't take them, only to have them take a tan one on the first drift. Thus, it seems more likely to me that the tan may also represent a dead scud, which at certain times of the year may be more commonly available than live ones that cling to the bottom. Alternatively, the Tan Scud may be a more accurate imitation of the natural olive-gray scud as seen through the trout's eye, which may perceive colors in a manner unlike our own. However, the most recent writings on the subject indicate that fish see colors much as we do. Perhaps the Tan Scud is a better imitation of the olive-gray scud as it appears at night during its behavioral drift.

Having posed what I think are reasonable questions about the trout's reaction to scuds, bear with me while I challenge the relevance of those questions. The Canyon trout take the Orange Scud best in May. The trout at Spinney take them from January through June. These are precisely the times when the rainbows spawn in these areas. Further, I have fished Orange Scuds to trout holding just downstream from spawning suckers and caught trout almost at will. I think the Orange Scud may be a fish-egg imitation. I wouldn't be surprised to learn that the tan ones imitate a week-old egg.

When I fish a Pheasant Tail Nymph, I know what I'm imitating. When I fish an Orange or Tan Scud, I really don't. As long as I'm catching trout, I don't get too bogged down by not knowing what I'm doing. However, if you solve the mystery of the scuds, please tell me the answer. I really would like to know why I'm catching all those fish.

WORMS

Yes, worms! There is an aquatic earthworm that lives in the muck under gravel areas in Cheesman Canyon and at Spinney. The worm

itself is a little lighter in color than a common red wiggler earthworm
and typically about two inches long. Trout love them. The naturals vary
in color, but all contain pink, gray, and brown. Ultrachenille tied to a
hook is all it takes for the fish to conclude that you've done a fine job
of imitating the natural. They are particularly effective in the spring and
during the high water of the runoff. Use enough weight to be certain
that the imitation is right on the bottom. Don't leave home without several
San Juan Worms, especially red, brown, and pink ones! This is a big
fly, but I hope you will be conscious of the damage that big hooks do
to trout and tie your San Juan Worms on a small hook such as a Mustad
3906, size 14. Please do not tie worm imitations on the large, curved
English bait hooks (Mustad 37160), which have a huge gape and ride
upside-down in the water. They hook a lot of trout in the brain.

EGGS

I was once called an elitist by a Colorado wildlife commissioner,
and I guess he's right. I don't like fishing egg imitations (Glo-Bugs)
because trout take them so deeply that I'm sure many die as a result.
I tie my Glo-Bugs on small hooks, Mustad 3906, size 14. I will fish Glo-
Bugs as a last resort, but I am very quick to set the hook. They are
primarily a springtime pattern, most effective when the rainbows are
spawning. Peach, orange, and chartreuse are the most effective colors.
Fish them with standard nymphing techniques. At the end of the dead
drift, slowly lift your rod tip in a Leisenring lift. Why trout should take
a rising Glo-Bug is another great mystery of the sport, but they do. If
you figure this one out please don't tell me; I really don't want to know.

MINNOWS

Trout everywhere will chase a minnow, which in the Platte may be
either small trout, small suckers, or fry of either. A black or olive-and-
black Woolly Bugger is effective most of the year. There must be abso-

lutely no insect activity for me to fish one, but when I do they usually work. I have pictures of a six-pound rainbow my son caught in a deep run in Cheesman Canyon during his spring break from school, shortly after I'd told him to "quit screwing around with that Woolly Bugger and come on up to the riffles where you can catch some fish." If you are after only big trout, the Woolly Bugger is the fly of choice. Cast it to the bank, down and across. Immediately after the fly lands, throw a downstream mend into the line to maximize the length of line perpendicular to the bank. Allow it to sink for several seconds followed by a retrieve of several short strips to pull the Bugger away from the bank, and then allow it to swing in the current. Olive Matukas are also effective.

I don't like to fish streamers because most times when I've been certain that a trout I had hooked was going to die, it had been hooked on a large streamer that had penetrated something other than its lip. Tie your streamers on small hooks (4X long shank, size 12) to avoid this problem. They work just as well.

TERRESTRIALS

Don't go to Cheesman Canyon without an orange ant, size 20. I've seen trout take them dry in February! Don't go to Spinney without a black beetle, size 18. During some years a yellow grasshopper also works well at Spinney. However, all the natural hoppers I've found there have been gray, about size 10 in August. The only hopper patterns I carry are yellow Letort Hoppers. At times the fish really hammer them. Perhaps they remember them in place of the golden stonefly adult that I don't bother to carry. A stonefly and a hopper should look a lot alike to a trout. Some year I'll be better prepared and tie some gray ones to test.

Fish terrestrials along the banks on hot afternoons when nothing else is going on. If you aren't successful matching the hatch, put on a beetle or an ant; you'll probably catch trout. Trout take them with a slow rise (except for hoppers), so don't set the hook too quickly. I have had some days at Spinney when a beetle produced as many fish as whatever was hatching that day. They regularly produce the biggest trout of the day. The trout don't underestimate terrestrials, and you shouldn't either.

6 Fishing Between the Hatches

Fishing between the hatches is really quite simple: You need to try nymphs, attractors, and terrestrials until you find something that works. A streamer is a last resort. This tactic is not as cumbersome as it sounds, as you know something about the river and what should be hatching at the time of year when you happen to be fishing. During the summer, all of these flies will work.

The nymphs the trout are used to seeing during the hatches will work before and after the hatches. For example, during the times of year when BWOs hatch, an RS-2 will work. When trout are seeing even occasional hatching caddis, Hare's Ear nymphs work well. Midges hatch in the Platte year-round; that's a good clue that a Quill Midge, Brassie, or Midge Larva should be among your first choices of nymphs. A red Midge Larva in size 18 is an excellent nymph at Spinney for much of the year. Usually, it is not a matter of only one nymph that will work, but of which one will work best. During the winter and spring, the Quill Midge, Midge Larva, Brassie, San Juan Worm, Glo-Bug, and scuds are the most likely to work, although RS-2s and Pheasant Tail Nymphs are sometimes effective.

During the summer months, imitations such as Pheasant Tail Nymphs, Hare's Ear Nymphs, Quill Midges, Brassies, tan scuds, green caddis larvae, and RS-2s will all work. Your only task is to find out what the trout want where you happen to be fishing. This is simply a matter of changing nymphs until you find the right one. Fish to visible trout and make sure you present your nymph at their depth. If you don't hook a trout after a dozen drifts, change nymphs.

There is a particular mind-set that we fishermen develop toward flies that have been successful for us in the past. We are loyal to them beyond all reason. It's fine to have a favorite nymph in which you have great confidence, but if it isn't working, admit it isn't working and try something else. Don't waste two hours trying to force-feed a Hare's Ear nymph to the trout if that isn't what they want. In my first half-hour on the stream, I may change flies six times before I find something the trout want.

Several tips for summer nymphing in Cheesman Canyon: Just after the sun drops low enough in the afternoon so that the water is shaded, tie on a Brassie. Midge activity or something must be triggered by the lack of direct sun, and you may take several trout within a few minutes. If you're not catching as many trout as you think you should be, perform the size test. Start with a size 18 nymph and work your way down until you find the size the trout want. If you get to size 26, use a Griffiths Gnat fished as a nymph (it is, after all, a peacock Woolly Worm). If you're still not catching trout, try the color test next. Try tan, gray, olive, and orange nymphs in rapid succession. You will sometimes discover that the trout are looking for a particular color, and these colors are the ones I have found that the trout in the Canyon sometimes key on. In the riffles, Pheasant Tail and Hare's Ear Nymphs (about size 18) always seem to work.

The most reliable nymphs for summer fishing at Spinney are the Pheasant Tail, the Green Machine, a small tan scud, and a red midge larva, about size 18. During high water when worms, crane fly larvae, and miscellaneous other food is dislodged from the bottom, San Juan Worms and other big nymphs work quite well. When the flow from either dam has been raised, try a San Juan Worm. Nymph fishing in the fall will use the same nymph selection, but the RS-2 and Quill Midge will be most likely to succeed.

Dry-fly action with attractors is good in both sections during June and July and typically lousy anytime but then. In Cheesman Canyon, fish Rio Grande King Trudes, sizes 10-12, and Adamses and Renegades, size 18. You should be in the Canyon early, about 6:00 A.M., to enjoy the best of the summer attractor fishing; it typically ends by 10:00 A.M. The edges of the river, slicks behind rocks, and the quiet eddies beside rocks are the most reliable spots.

The attractors that are most useful below Spinney are the Royal Wulff and parachute Royal Wulff, Adams, and Renegade, all in size 18.

Fish the Wulffs in the riffles and the other two in quiet water along the banks. A large Griffiths Gnat (size 16) is also an effective attractor here. Two of my favorite attractors are the PMD emerger and the Devil Bug, both size 18. I fish them the same way anyone else would fish an Adams, and they will bring up trout when nothing is hatching. June and July have good morning hatches, so attractor fishing is something to do during afternoons when you're not in the mood to fish nymphs.

Fish orange ants (#20) in Cheesman Canyon all summer long. Fish beetles (#18) below Spinney during June and July. Both should be fished along the banks. Pull the ant under at the end of its drag-free drift and let it swing as a wet fly; the trout sometimes prefer it fished wet. Fish hoppers at Spinney during August and September, but with the expectation that some years the trout will see so few hoppers that they will not work. Too much wet spring weather promotes the growth of a fungus that may kill the hopper eggs and reduce the summer hopper population. Even though Spinney is a meadow area, the hopper is not my favorite terrestrial.

Woolly Buggers and other streamers work best when the trout feed actively for most of the day, usually June and July. Do not discount their effectiveness at other times, though: Big trout may chase one anytime between March and November.

Schaum's Outline

As a college student, I often found myself facing a test the next day in some course I disliked, not having cracked the text for that course in the past month. My solution to the predicament was to go to the bookstore, buy the *Schaum's Outline* for the subject and spend three hours that evening studying the appropriate sections of that outline. That was always enough to get me through the exam in a passable, occasionally respectable manner. This chapter is "Schaum's Outline" of the South Platte. You won't gain any understanding by reading it, but you can look at it the night before, check your fly boxes, tie a half-dozen needed flies, and expect to demonstrate passable, occasionally respectable fish-catching skills the next day.

First, I present "the year in review"—what works when. Second, I list the various flies you will use through the course of the year, in case you're one of those plan-ahead types.

January through March

Nymphs: Muskrat #22-26, Pheasant Tail #20, Quill Midge #20-26, red midge larva #18, RS-2 #18, San Juan Worm, scuds.

Dry Flies: Griffiths Gnat, No-Name Midge, Stillborn Midge; all #22-28.

April and May

Nymphs: Same as for January-March, but Brassies, the Orange Scud, and the RS-2 will be particularly effective; add dark Hare's Ear soft-hackle in mid-May.

Dry Flies: Same as for January-March, but add BWO imitations #18-22; in particular conventional Blue Quills, Comparaduns, floating nymphs, and Rusty Spinners.

June

Nymphs: Hare's Ear #18, Pheasant Tail #18, RS-2 #18, San Juan Worm, tan scuds.

Dry Flies: Comparaduns #16, Fore-and-Aft #16, PMD emergers #18 at Spinney; Adams #20-26, Devil Bug #20-26, Elk Hair Caddis #20-26, Griffiths Gnat #20-26, No-Name Midge #20-26, Renegade #20-26, Rio Grande King Trude #20-26, Stillborn Midge #20-26.

July

Nymphs: Add Green Machine #22-24 to June's list.

Dry Flies: Add Comparaduns, floating nymphs, spinners, and Trico emergers, all #24, to June's list; orange ant should be #20 and PMDs #18-20 in Canyon; black beetle and Royal Wulff #18 at Spinney.

August through September

Nymphs: Nymphing will be slow; I generally fish the Tricos and go home.

Dry Flies: Ants, beetles, some midges, Trico patterns; add Letort Hopper #10 at Spinney.

October through November

Nymphs: RS-2 #18-20 is your best bet.

Dry Flies: BWO imitations (see April).

December

Nymphs: Aren't the Broncos playing today?

Dry Flies: If I thought trout were rising, I wouldn't be watching football.

The following list includes what I consider to be the minimum essential set of flies required to fish the Platte through the course of the year. Every expert will complain that I have omitted his most important imitation, but I suspect that *something* on my list will serve the same purpose.

Dry Flies

Adams #18-22

Black beetle #18

Dark Comparadun #18-24 (gray, dark olive, or brown)
Devil Bug #18-20
Elk Hair Caddis #16-20 (with and without hackle, light and dark)
Emerger #18-24
Floating nymph #18-24
Fore-and-Aft #16-18 (black), #18 (quill body), #20 (green)
Griffiths Gnat #22-28 (also fish as nymph)
Hackle Wing Spinner #18-20 (rust), #22-26 (black)
Letort Hopper #10
Light Comparadun #16-20 (yellow, light olive, or tan)
No-Name Midge #22-26
Orange ant #20
Renegade #18
Rio Grande King Trude #10-14
Royal Wulff #18 (also parachute #16-18)
Stillborn Midge #22-26

Nymphs

Brassie #18-24 (also fish dry)
Dark Hare's Ear soft-hackle #16-22 (also fish dry)
Green Machine #20-24 (also fish dry)
Midge larva #18-22 (white), #16-18 (red)
Muskrat nymph #22-26 (also fish dry)
Quill Midge #20-26 (also fish dry)
Pheasant Tail #16-20
RS-2 #18-24 (gray), #14-18 (tan), #16-24 (olive)
San Juan Worm #12 (red, brown, pink)
Scuds #12-16 (orange, tan, and olive-gray; TMC 2487 hook)

Streamers

Woolly Bugger #12 (olive and black or black tied long)

Courtesy and Ethics

If you're just starting to fly fish, one of the most important things to learn is not to spoil someone else's fun. The good fishermen I know are generous with their flies and advice to someone who asks questions but doesn't crowd them or scare the trout they are stalking. If you want to ask someone a question, do so from a position fifty feet behind them and you are certain to get the information you asked for. In particular, stay back from the banks as you are walking to a new spot so that you will not spook the trout near the banks that a fellow fisherman may be attempting to catch. Pay particular attention to a fellow fisherman's actions, whether working upstream, downstream, or staying in one spot. Do not move a short distance past him and then begin fishing to the trout he would have reached in only a few minutes. If you have even the slightest doubt as to whether you're crowding someone, ask before you do so. On crowded days in particular, the good fishermen are more likely to invite the courteous fisherman to share a good spot, knowing that good conversation, comparison of notes on what is working, and other companionable activities are better than being crowded by a poor sport. On such days, we must all make room for everyone, and none of us has a right to one hundred yards of river for our exclusive enjoyment. When it is crowded, be a good sport about allowing others to fish near you without snide comments or tantrums, unless you are the victim of blatant poor sportsmanship.

If you're fortunate enough to get a really good spot, after you've caught a reasonable number of trout either move on and allow someone else to fish it or, at the very least, offer to share it with others. In the winter in particular, the trout collect in only a few places, and if

you are to catch anything, it will be from one of those spots. The height
of poor sportsmanship is to park in such a spot, catch fish after fish,
and not allow anyone else the pleasure of catching a few. If you've caught
a half-dozen trout from any spot, be a good sport and move on.

Finally, don't be passive to the point of allowing those ignorant of
fishing etiquette to spoil your fun. If you're casting to a big trout holding
beside a bank and someone is about to walk within a few feet of your
trout, say something! At least once a day I find myself saying, "I've got
a fish on the bank I really want to catch. I'd sure appreciate it if you
would move well back from the bank before you go by. Thanks." I've
encountered only one person who voiced any displeasure with my polite
request. The one who did was not a spin fisherman, but a conspicuously
yuppie fly fisherman who arrogantly informed me that the trout in the
South Platte are impossible to spook. I wasn't inclined to explain to him
how to cope with spooky trout feeding selectively on #26 midges while
hatching BWOs are still on the surface, and neither is anyone else. It's
his loss. If you are trying to learn the Platte, the good fishermen there
will teach you as they did me, but only if you are one of the true gentlemen of the sport.

Ethical behavior on-stream is like saving for retirement. If you want
to enjoy the future rather than merely endure it, you must plan for that
now. Colorado is growing; the crowds on our streams will only get bigger.
If you want to enjoy the South Platte in the future you will have to do
your part to protect and enhance it *now!* That includes doing whatever
you can to minimize damage to either the trout or the stream and, when
you find others damaging either, say something. I don't suggest you
risk your life to tell a motorcycle gang to take their worms and leave,
but there is a phone number on your license so you can report such
violations to someone who is well prepared to deal with them.

One of the most persistent and objectionable violations of ethical
fishing behavior is the "San Juan shuffle." It is not unusual to see so-
called nymph fishermen shuffling their feet to dislodge nymphs from
the stream bottom and then drifting their nymphs downstream into the
collection of trout feeding just below where they stand. Such charac-
ters claim to "catch" many trout. Unfortunately, most of their trout are
foul hooked, and many will suffer or die as a result. The habitat of the
insects is also damaged. These "fishermen" threaten our future fun and

should be told that they are not sportsmen for doing the shuffle. What their selfish actions demonstrate is their ability to snag fish in a barrel, nothing more. Conscientious sportsmen should continue to encourage the Division of Wildlife and the Wildlife Commission to outlaw this destructive practice.

Fishing a barbless hook is such an obvious means of reducing the handling required to release trout that I wonder why it isn't required by regulations. The excuse given by the Division of Wildlife is that the research indicates no difference in hooking mortality between barbless and barbed hooks. This research is done with hatchery fish by trained personnel who can quickly remove a hook and properly release the fish. What I see on the stream are inexperienced fishermen squeezing a trout to hold it still, dropping it on the bank to search for a pair of pliers, and then struggling to remove the hook while again squeezing the trout. Once the hook is removed the trout is simply tossed back into the river without being revived. These are vastly different conditions from the research conditions. It is apparent to anyone on the stream that barbless hooks that are easily removed will lead to reduced hooking mortality.

When you do catch that big trout I hope you will release it, even if the regulations where the trout was caught would allow you to kill it. None of us catch enough big trout and I would like the opportunity to catch it also. Some other fisherman may have returned it for you to catch. You can thank him by allowing someone else to catch it too. Furthermore, that trout succeeded very well in its habitat, and the stream needs its genes if there are to be more like it for our future fun.

Finally, I hope you will give something back to the sport that provides you so much enjoyment. The most effective single thing you can do to promote good fishing is to attend Wildlife Commission meetings and write letters to wildlife commissioners, the Division of Wildlife, and politicians to let them know your views on the issues that affect us, our trout, and our rivers. They make the day-to-day decisions that affect our sport, but they work for us. Be a good boss and let them know what you expect of them. The future of our sport depends on it.

9

March 18, 1989: A Word About Two Forks

I didn't plan to meet Reg and Dick until eight, and I always awaken by six. I had plenty of time to get some sleep if I could only fall asleep. It's not uncommon for me to be too excited to sleep well the night before a fishing trip, particularly early in the season as this was, but this was ridiculous. The events of the day passed through my mind over and over; I just couldn't believe what had happened. Finally, at 4:30 A.M. I went out for the newspapers, three of them, and read all about it. In fact, I had read all about it three or four times by the time I met Reg and Dick for the drive to the Canyon.

I've always been in a hurry to get into the Canyon. When I first started fly fishing I was also doing the Pikes Peak ascent race every year, and running into the Canyon with a backpack filled with my gear was great training. When Reg and I started fishing together he would occasionally ask, "Are we about to miss the hatch?" What he meant was that there was really no reason to make a one-mile walk over a steep hill in ten minutes instead of twenty.

I've finally learned that ten minutes will not make or break a day of fishing. Still, time in the Canyon has always seemed too short, too infrequent, much like the time you spend with an old dog that you know you won't have much longer. In only a few short years, maybe less, he will be gone—and so would the Canyon, I felt. This morning, however, I was content to hike at an amble, noticing how blue a young blue spruce really is, that pine bark can be rust or black, that black pointy-eared squirrels really aren't all that rare, and that the sun had never, until this very day, shone as bright!

Reg tells a lot of other fishermen that the only reason he fishes with

61

me is that when we get there, I have my gear on and have figured out what the trout want before he even has his waders unpacked. Instead of puzzling over what the trout want, all he has to do is ask me! The first part is usually true and the second part occasionally true, but this morning he had released a fish ten minutes before I was ready to start. I was in real danger of having someone mistake me for a Type B personality. We continued talking about the events of the day before until we drifted apart. At the time, all three of us were fishing #22 Quill Midges and taking occasional trout, but none of us was trying very hard to catch much other than a cold.

I had received the news the day before when Karl Licis (the outdoor sports editor for the *Colorado Springs Gazette Telegraph*) called and asked what I thought. The Environmental Protection Agency had scheduled a news conference for 1:00 P.M., and it was about noon when he called. "Haven't you heard? They're announcing a veto of Two Forks." I was as near dumbstruck as a salesman ever is, but I still managed to give him a reasonably intelligent comment for his story. I spent the rest of the afternoon on the telephone, talking to everyone I knew who had been interested in the issue.

A lot of us who fish the Canyon had been going to hearings about the proposed Two Forks Dam for the better part of five years. The Army Corps of Engineers was charged with assessing the environmental impacts of new water projects for the Denver metropolitan area, and they conducted regular hearings seeking citizen input on such projects. Even prior to the application to build Two Forks, it was clear that the attendees at those hearings were against that project and equally clear that the Metropolitan Water Providers wouldn't seriously consider any alternative. After the application for Two Forks was filed, the hearings changed in character. Those opposed to Two Forks turned out to include not just fishermen and a few dedicated others but everyone from sweet little old ladies who once picnicked at Deckers to irate property owners who live there, as broad a cross section of people as you will find in a supermarket on Saturday morning. Fishermen were only a small part of the opposition to Two Forks. The hearings often had the character of a high school pep rally, with wild cheering for statements opposing Two Forks. The Metropolitan Water Providers and politicians were always allowed to speak first on the need for Two Forks, followed by comments from the attendees who wanted to speak. The comments from the public usually ran about 95 percent opposed to issuing a permit for the construction of Two Forks.

Both sides of the Two Forks issue were well organized and well prepared. Environmental organizations opposed to Two Forks had previously formed a coalition to magnify and coordinate their individual efforts. Groups ranging from the Audubon Society to Trout Unlimited rallied their members to action against the dam. The issues were argued in the fashion of a political campaign. Much of the argument was conducted for the benefit of the press. Those supporting Two Forks always seemed to exaggerate the dire consequences of not building it (brown lawns, brown parks, dead golf courses, recession, and so on) and acted as if there were no alternatives. The environmentalists often exaggerated their case, too. At one hearing I attended, an Earth First! member even promised to lie down in front of the bulldozers and to dynamite the dam during its construction. Emotions on both sides ran high. Letters were sent by the thousands to the Corps of Engineers, mostly opposing Two Forks. From the beginning, the supporters of the dam relied on sympathetic politicians to pressure the Corps in every way they could. Governor Roy Romer was asked by the Corps of Engineers to provide a statement of his position on building the dam. He came out squarely for both sides of the issue, asking that the permit be issued but opposing the building of it. That straddle earned him criticism from both sides, although his statement that he wanted to find an alternative to Two Forks was in reality a victory for the environmental community.

The mainstream of the environmental coalition never argued that the Denver metropolitan area didn't need additional water for the future, but rather that there were alternatives that didn't create the environmental destruction of Two Forks. The Metropolitan Water Providers attempted to frame the issue as growth versus no-growth in an economically depressed state. In the end, the public was fairly well educated and opposed to Two Forks. Finally, the Corps of Engineers found it to be in the public interest to issue a permit to build Two Forks. Attention then shifted to the Environmental Protection Agency (EPA), which had final authority to allow or veto the issuance of the permit to build the dam.

The environmental coalition efforts were led by the Environmental Defense Fund under the direction of Dr. Dan Luecke, a hydrologist who understood the water issues as well as or better than anyone in the employ of the Metropolitan Water Providers. Throughout the entire process, he presented the alternatives to the Corps and the EPA. The Water Providers continued to press their case with the EPA, which is headed in the Denver region by an appointee having a background in state politics. Letters flowed to the EPA as they had to the Corps earlier, and in about the same ratio for and against. Leaks to the press indicated that the EPA technical staff was opposed to permitting the building of Two Forks, but that the regional administrator was prepared to issue the permit. In the meantime, luck intervened. We elected George Bush as president, and he in turn appointed William Reilly as head of the EPA.

Mr. Reilly has a background as head of an environmental organization, and one of his first actions was to remove the Two Forks permit decision from the Denver Regional Office of the EPA. His next decision was to initiate the veto process for the Two Forks permit. This decision was announced on March 17, 1989. The Metropolitan Water Providers howled in indignation and began political pressure to reverse the decision at a higher level, this time with the president's chief of staff, John Sununu. To his credit, President Bush was resolute that the Two Forks decision was to be made by the EPA, not in the White House. Again, the process continued with the environmental community, the Metropolitan Water Providers, and the public expressing their views to the Washington, D.C., office of the EPA and the president. The EPA had its regional administrator from Atlanta study the issues, and he too recommended that the veto process continue. The deputy EPA administrator for water issues then continued the process and reached the same conclusion. On November 23, 1990, a veto of the proposed dam at the Two Forks site was issued. Among the reasons for the veto were the unacceptable damages to fishery and recreational areas that would be caused by the construction of a dam at Two Forks. The good guys finally won!

There are many factors behind the defeat of Two Forks. First, there are better and cheaper ways to solve the Denver water problem than Two Forks. That fact is obvious to anyone who has spent as much as a few hours reading the various summaries of the environmental impact statements, although many of our politicians were unwilling to do even that. Second, the environmental coalition could not have chosen a better spokesman than Dan Luecke; always smooth, always in control of the facts, always arguing the facts, not the emotions, of the issue. On the other hand, the Metropolitan Water Providers made very poor choices of both tactics and spokesmen; always shrill, always alarmist, alienating by undue pressure even those they sought to persuade. Third, luck played a major role. If the environmental impact statement had not taken so long, the previous head of the EPA would surely not have stopped Two Forks. In the end, credit for the defeat of Two Forks must go mostly to those who took the time to write a letter, sit through a hearing, or call a politician; it was the little people who stopped a giant dam and saved a beautiful playground for us and our kids. Having stopped Two Forks, we little people must now use our power responsibly to create an acceptable equivalent.

The sun was warm that day, but the fishing was not. The water was really cold, and I was tired of having numb feet. There is one particular spot where I usually do well with nymphs, two plunge pools on either side of a gravel bar. I walked toward that spot more to warm my feet than out of a desire to catch any more trout. A single trout rose at the head of the gravel bar as I crossed the current downstream from it. I instinctively dropped to my knees and crept closer. I had been hoping to take a trout on the surface that day, so the first thing I tried was removing the split shot from my leader and floating the Quill Midge nymph over the trout. Several times it appeared to take but turned away. I needed more tippet and something smaller than the #22 I was fishing. It was early enough in the year that I had not yet stocked my flyboxes for the season. The smallest dry fly I could find was a #24 Griffiths Gnat, which was given similar treatment by the trout. Finally, I found a shredded midge pupa, a #26 that I had returned to the far corner of my flybox so that I could tie a new fly on that valuable Partridge hook. The trout took it on the first drift, my first trout on the surface for 1989. It was an ordinary Canyon brown, about twelve inches, and as wild, beautiful, and satisfying as any trout I've ever caught.

I spent the rest of the afternoon sitting on a rock, enjoying the warm sunshine and the nip in the air. The last fish had been a challenge, but I was in no hurry to find that satisfaction again. I knew the Canyon would always be there. I could always go back.

I enjoyed the feeling of having the Canyon forever for perhaps a month. When I found myself once again writing letters to politicians and the EPA about Two Forks, I realized that the Platte will always be under attack. Politics can change any political decision, and although the intensity of the attack will wax and wane, it will not end. I was fifty years old as this went to press, and I expect to fight Two Forks again in my lifetime. I took the time to write this and have donated the royalties to Trout Unlimited. I've opened my flybox to you, told you all my secrets. Maybe all this will help get you hooked on the Platte. If so, when we fight Two Forks again you'll be there to help, and my time will have been well spent, indeed.

10 Special Flies of the South Platte

The biggest challenge you will face in tying the special flies of the Platte is learning to tie small but sparse flies. There are a few tips that will help you with this effort, and I present them here in random order. Following my tying tips are recipes for the important but less commonly known flies you will need. The numbers of tails or wing fibers I give were learned by trial and error. If you have to repeat those experiments, go ahead, but please try it my way once before you tell me that my patterns don't work. I tell you numbers because that is what works best for me. Similarly, if a recipe does not call for a tail on a pattern, don't put a tail on it! Finally, for me, tying flies is a necessary evil, not a pleasure. I tie only simple, durable flies. If a fly takes more than five minutes to tie, or won't last for fifty fish, I won't carry it. Thus, you will find that my tying instructions occasionally include extra cement to improve the durability of the flies. You may omit it if you wish.

Dubbing Needle

Commercial dubbing needles are not fine enough to cement tiny heads without getting head cement in the eye. Make your own by pressing the eye of a very fine sewing needle into the end of a quarter-inch dowel rod about six inches long with a pair of pliers. Secure it with a drop of Superglue (thin cyanoacrylate cement). Be careful with this stuff! (See "Quill Bodies" below.)

69

Head Cement

Every time I go to a fishing show I gag as some macho commercial tyer says his flies will stay together without cement. He's usually tying a size 10 pattern of some sort, which he finishes with six half-hitches and three whip finishes. They probably do stay together, but the head he is tying is larger than many of the flies you need for the Platte. Ignore these guys!

I use *thinned* Dave's Flexament as head cement. It is strong! Whip-finish the heads on small flies using only five turns and light thread tension. Tighten the knot gently, but do not trim yet. After dipping your new dubbing needle into head cement, touch the tip of the needle to your left thumbnail to leave only a tiny drop on the needle. Lift the bobbin with your left hand to bring the thread horizontal to the whip finish, and then hold the needle vertically and slide the middle of the needle along the thread until it touches the fly. Slide the needle up until the cement drop touches the rear turns of the whip finish. If you need more cement, it's there on your thumbnail. Trim tag to about 1/16″ long. The tag should be saturated with cement. This procedure should allow you to cement the heads on even tiny flies without getting cement in the eye of the hook. If you do, clean it immediately with your dubbing needle or you'll never be able to tie that fly to a tippet.

Hackle Pliers

Buy the smallest teardrop hackle pliers you can find. This style grips tightly without cutting or breaking tiny hackle stems.

Vise

Whatever vise you like, midge jaws will improve it.

Herl Bodies or Collars

Whenever a recipe calls for herl, the portion of the hook shank underlying the herl should be covered with thread. Soak that portion of the thread with head cement immediately before winding the herl over it.

Split Tails

Many mayfly imitations call for split tails. Most of the flies that do are too small to use a ball of dubbing to split the tails and still produce a properly proportioned body. Use the tying thread to split the tails as follows: Tie on the tail fibers and wind the thread smoothly to the bend of the hook. Bring the thread under the tail fibers and pull forward to flare the tails. Use your dubbing needle to divide the tail fibers into two clumps having equal numbers of fibers. Pull these clumps to either side of the shank with your fingers. Bring the tying thread under the hook shank, then up between the two clumps, then over the shank. Pull forward to adjust the flare of the near clump, then wrap one turn around the shank slightly forward of the base of the tails. Hold your dubbing needle horizontally 1/2" above the hook shank at the rear of the fly, pointed directly away from your chest. Bring the tying thread over the needle, then between the hook shank and the far tail clump. Slowly lower and then remove the dubbing needle as you pull the thread forward until the flare of the far clump is as desired. Wind two more wraps. If the fly is a large one, you may wish to bring the dubbed thread through the tail clumps as above, although it is not necessary. It takes a lot longer to explain how to do this than it does to just do it at the vise.

Little Stuff

When you are handling or tying on something that is very tiny, hold it with hackle pliers. Use hackle pliers to remove tiny hackles from the rooster neck. Grip them at their attachment at the skin, and you can easily remove one at a time without breaking them. Then hold the hackle with the pliers as you tie it in.

Quill Bodies

Remove the herl fibers from peacock herls by rubbing them with a pencil eraser. Soak stripped peacock herl in water for at least fifteen minutes before you attempt to wind it. Tie in, wind forward, and tie off using very little thread tension for the first wrap. Cover the body with Superglue to strengthen it. Remove the excess from the body with your dubbing needle, but do not wipe the needle with your fingers to clean it, use a kleenex. Superglue will do an excellent job of gluing your fingers together or to whatever you touch next! Be careful with this stuff; if you get it in your eyes, a trip to the emergency room is the most important thing on your agenda.

Biot Bodies

Biot bodies are all the rage for midge imitations. They really don't work any better than anything else for me, but they really catch fishermen. To tie with them, first soak a clump of biots in water for about twenty to thirty minutes. Hold one biot by its tip and look at the butt end. It is L-shaped. Lay the biot on your table and cut it approximately in half lengthwise with a single-edge razor blade, keeping the part with the short part of the L. This is the part that creates the fuzzy rib. Tie in the tip of the biot at the rear of the hook, with the fuzzy edge up. Grip the biot with a hackle pliers and take one turn of the biot around the shank to see if the rib stands up. If it does not, the biot must be wound in the opposite direction around the shank. Coat the shank with head cement, wind the biot forward, and tie off. All the biots from that clump will wind in the same direction.

Thread and Thread Tension

I use 8/0 thread for all of the small flies for the Platte. When you are tying something onto a tiny fly, use very light thread tension for two wraps, followed by one or two tighter wraps to secure it.

Dubbing

Use dubbing wax. I prefer muskrat and beaver for dries. I prefer to blend several colors together for most dubbings. Learn to pull three or four fibers at a time from the dubbing clump so that you dub only tiny amounts onto the thread for small flies.

Soft Hackles

I tie soft-hackle flies down to size 26 using the following technique: Select a small feather from the part of a bird wing that corresponds to your shoulder. Grip the very tip of the feather with the tip of the smallest hackle pliers you can obtain, and then stroke the fibers back along the stem. Find the area of the stem where the fibers are the proper length, and trim off all the fibers beyond this point that are too long. Stroke the fibers that are too short toward the tip, leaving a band of fibers about 3/16" wide on each side of the stem. You will now be holding, with your hackle pliers, a feather having a band of fibers sticking out perpendicularly from the stem and others pointing toward the tip of the feather.

Tie it onto the head of the hook at the separation of the fiber clumps, with the tip of the feather pointing back. Dub the body, and then carefully wrap two turns of the feather. As you wind the feather, twist the hackle pliers as required to keep most of the feather fibers pointing perpendicularly to the hook shank. Tie off and trim the feather butt. Push the feather fibers back with a half-hitch tool, and hold with your left hand as you wrap several turns in front of the hackle. Whip-finish and cement.

MAYFLY IMITATIONS

Emerger

Hook: TMC 100, #18-24
Thread: brown or olive
Abdomen: pheasant tail or olive brown fur
Thorax: hare's ear with lots of guard hair
Wing case: elk hair, deer hair, or poly yarn

Tie in several pheasant tail herls by their tips, wind thread to bend of
hook, wrap herls several turns counterclockwise around thread, and
wind forward to head of fly. Tie off and trim. Cut a small clump of elk
or deer hair, hold by tips in your left hand, and tie in at thorax using
light thread tension. Do not crush hair tightly. Dub thorax, then pull
hair forward over thorax and secure to head with several wraps. Lift hair

clump and stand up with several more thread wraps. Whip-finish and cement. Trim hair clump to one-third length of shank.

• Grease only the front tuft when you fish this fly.

You and I will be forever indebted to Al Cohen, a Dallas salmon fly tyer of some note, who showed me his emerger pattern on the banks of DePuys Spring Creek in July 1983.

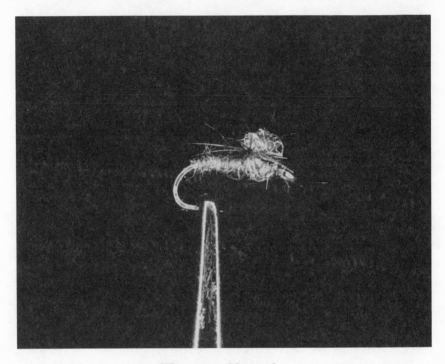

Floating Nymph

Hook: TMC 100, #18-24
             TMC 2487, #14-22
Thread: brown or olive
Abdomen: medium brown fur
Hackle: one or two turns brown or dark dun, wrapped Parachute-
             style around wing case
Wing case: dark gray, poly dubbing

Wax your fingers with dubbing wax, and then tightly dub small amounts
of poly dubbing onto thread in a section about 3/8″ long. Twist dubbing
first across thread, then along thread to shorten dubbed section into
a football shape. Hold bobbin above hook shank one-third of the shank
length back from head. Slide dubbing down to hook, then hold dubbing
ball gently with left hand. Bring thread around shank, then gently pull
slack from thread. Wrap several wraps in front and back of dubbing ball

and several wraps horizontally around the base of the ball. Tie in hackle butt just behind the ball with hackle tip pointing forward. Wrap two more turns around base of ball and hackle. Dub body, using figure-eight wraps under thorax. Wind hackle one or two turns counterclockwise around ball and tie off hackle on head. Trim hackle fibers from front of fly. Whip-finish and cement.

• Grease only the hackle and wing case when you fish this fly.

This is Gary Borger's adaptation of the Swisher-Richards Floating Nymph. He showed me this fly in 1983 on the banks of DePuys Spring Creek. I've had few problems with mayfly hatches since that memorable trip.

Comparadun

Hook: TMC 100, #16-26
Thread: to match body
Abdomen: fine dyed fur, preferably beaver or muskrat
Wing: fine deer hair or dyed elk hair
Tails: two, four, or six Micro Fibetts, depending on size of fly

The trick to Comparaduns is finding the proper hair. You do not want deer-mask or elk-hock. Obtain fine deer hair that is about one inch long and will flare. Do not try long, coarse deer hair as it just doesn't work. Tie tails onto front of hook shank, wind thread to center of shank, then wind forward to a point one-fourth of shank length back from the eye. Cut a small clump of hair, remove underfur, and stack. Hold hair clump in left hand, with tips pointing forward. Your left thumb and index finger should squeeze the clump with the length pointing forward equal to the shank length. From this point on, *do not let go of the hair until I tell you to!* Hold the hair over the shank pointing to your right, take one loose wrap over the hair at what will become the base of the wing, and slowly tighten the thread until the hair flares. Wrap four tight turns smoothly toward the bend of the hook. Pull butts of hair up, then trim as close to the thread wraps as possible. *Hold your left hand over a wastebasket and let go of the hair.* Smoothly wrap thread forward to base of wing. Stand up wing with half-hitch tool, then again hold with left hand as you wrap about ten turns in front of wing to secure it in a vertical position. Put a generous drop of head cement into the base of the wing. Wrap thread to rear of hook, split tails, apply dubbing very sparsely, whip-finish and cement. Spread hair fibers into a 180-degree fan about top of hook shank.

I use yellow-dyed beaver for PMDs and mixed (dyed) olive and brown beaver for BWOs. For Tricos, I use gray muskrat with a tiny pinch of black fur for the thorax. Use six Micro Fibetts for size 16, four for sizes 18-20, two for sizes 22-26.

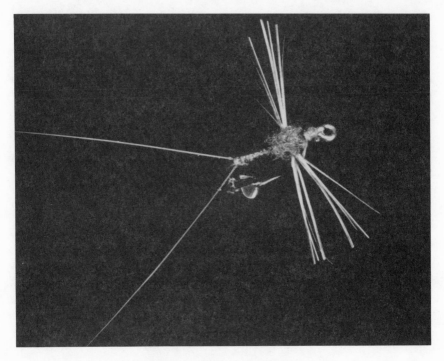

Hackle-Wing Spinner

Hook: TMC 100, #18-26
Thread: brown or black to match body
Abdomen: tying thread, coated with head cement
Thorax: rusty or black fur or poly dubbing
Wing: eight hackle fibers
Tails: two Micro Fibetts

Tie on Micro Fibetts, wind thread to bend of hook, and split tails. Wind thread forward to a point one-third of the hook-shank length back from the eye. Select a large but not webby hackle feather from a dun or grizzly rooster neck. Trim four fibers from a point near the tip of the hackle and lay them on the base of your vise with about 1/4″ extending over the edge. Trim four more fibers from the hackle and lay them over the first bunch, but with the tips pointed in the opposite direction. Carefully pick up and tie hackle fibers onto shank with figure-eight wraps. Trim wings to shank length, push both wings upward to flare the fibers slightly, then wind two wraps through the wing fiber clumps using very light thread tension. Adjust thread tension to flare the wings into a 30-40-degree fan. Apply a generous amount of head cement to the wing base and all thread on the fly. Apply dubbing to thread and wind over wing base in figure-eight wraps, top and bottom, to form a spherical thorax about one-fourth shank length in diameter. Whip-finish and cement.

This wing is the only original idea in this book, and I suspect a thousand others before me have already invented it.

Some fishermen like their Trico spinners tied with a peacock herl thorax. Others swear by an olive abdomen. Plain black is all I've ever needed.

RS-2

Hook: TMC 100, #18-24
Thread: to match body
Body: sparsely dubbed fur, various colors
Wing case: clump of down from the base of a pheasant body feather, or
            black antron yarn
Tails: two beaver guard hairs, split

This is probably the single most effective fly for Cheesman Canyon. It works in gray, tan, brown, and olive. If you want to make it fancy you can tie the wing case in a little behind the head and dub a head in front of it. It is easier just to tie the wing case in at the head. It is a matter of considerable indifference to the trout.

This pattern is one from a series of patterns invented by Rim Chung, a Denver tyer. Its name is from "Rim, Style 2."

MIDGE IMITATIONS

Fore-and-Aft

Hook: TMC 100, #18-22
Thread: to match body
Abdomen: fur or poly dubbing, herl, or quill
Hackle: dun, two or three turns at head and rear of fly

I imitate the big midge using black herl from the tip of a wild turkey tail feather. Wrap the herl around the tying thread several turns counterclockwise before winding the body forward. Stripped peacock quill is also effective. Use green dubbing to imitate mating green midges.

John Riley showed me this fly with a quill body, and it has become one of my favorite dry flies.

Griffiths Gnat

Hook: Partridge K1A, #24-28
            TMC 100, #22-26
            TMC 501, #20-24
Thread: black
Body: peacock herl
Hackle: grizzly, three or four turns; palmer

You don't need any help with this one.

Stillborn Midge

Hook: Partridge K1A, #24-28
                TMC 100, #22-26
                TMC 501, #20-24
Thread: black
Thorax: peacock herl, or omit
Hackle: grizzly, two turns; palmer; grease before fishing
Shuck: tuft of muskrat fur; take care not to grease

Hold a tuft of muskrat fur tightly, trim from skin, and remove guard hairs. Measure to length slightly longer than shank, and then tie onto middle of shank with several tight wraps. Trim butts close to thread. Put a drop of head cement into the butts of the muskrat fur after trimming. Tie a very short Griffiths Gnat on remaining forward portion of shank. This high-tech midge emerger is really a Woolly Bugger, nothing more. I gave you a lot of hook choices. Just make sure you have some *little* ones.

No-Name Midge/Conventional Midge

Hook: Partridge K1A, #24-28
            TMC 100, #22-26
            TMC 501, #20-24
Thread: to match body
Body: fur, quill, or biot
Hackle: two turns (see below)
Tail: none, or three Micro Fibetts for conventional midge

My favorite hackle/body combinations are grizzly/muskrat, grizzly/quill, and dun/olive fur or olive biot. You don't need all of these; you just need a good selection of sizes. I usually tie them with tails and trim them off on stream if the trout don't like the tail. You may also find that removing the tail and trimming the hackle flat under the shank will sometimes improve its effectiveness; this variation allows the body to be under the mirror where it is more visible to the trout.

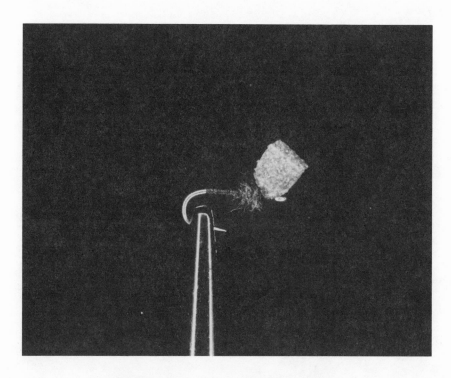

Midge Pupa/Suspender Midge

Hook: Partridge K1A, #24-28
            TMC 100, #22-26
            TMC 501, #20-24
Abdomen: tying thread
Thorax: loosely dubbed fur
Suspender: none, or closed-cell gray foam 1/8" thick or a dubbing ball
            as on floating nymph

A Suspender Midge is a midge pupa tied with a ball of foam at the head. Cut a strip of closed-cell foam about 1/8" square and tie in at head. Trim closely behind head and about 1/8" in front of eye. Wrap thread to bend of hook and then back to head. Dub a prominent but shaggy thorax. Tie off and cement. My favorite colors for thread/thorax combination are black/darkest bronze beaver and olive/gray muskrat.

Fish the Suspender as a dry, greasing only the foam. Fish the pupa every way that works.

I tie most of my Midge Pupae as Suspenders and trim off Suspender foam if I need to fish the fly under the surface.

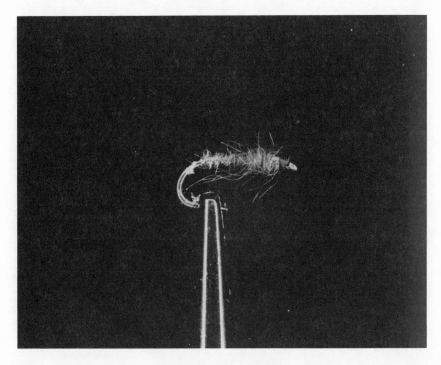

Muskrat Nymph

Hook: TMC 100, #20-26
Thread: gray
Body: muskrat fur, very sparse

Build up thorax with tying thread, sparsely dub thread, and wind onto hook. Whip-finish and cement. This is my kind of fly!

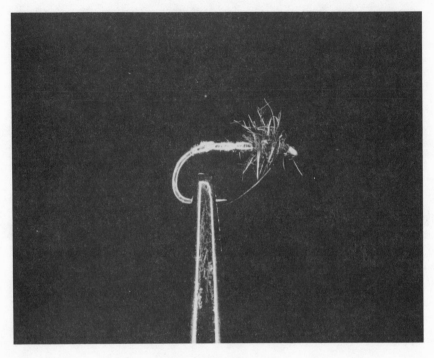

Brassie

Hook:	TMC 100, #18-26
Thread:	black
Body:	ribbon copper wire
Collar:	hare's ear, peacock, or ostrich herl

Buy a helical telephone cord from Radio Shack—one of those curly ones that run from the telephone receiver to the handpiece. Cut a one-turn length and remove the four colored wires from the white outer case. Carefully strip the insulation from one of these, then untwist the four ribbon wires from around their inner core. Tie a copper ribbon onto the hook shank and wind thread first to rear of hook and then forward, using very little thread tension. Wind ribbon forward. Tie off using very little thread tension, then work copper ribbon back and forth to trim. Coat copper with head cement. Apply collar; whip-finish and cement.

Don't tie more than a half-dozen of these at a time, because they tarnish in about a month and become ineffective.

This nymph was shown to me years ago by Steve Johnson, as skilled a nymph fisherman as any who have waded the Platte.

Quill Midge (Midge Pupa)

Hook: TMC 100, #18-26
Thread: black
Body: stripped peacock herl
Collar: hare's ear, muskrat, peacock, or ostrich herl

Midge Larva (String Thing)

Hook: TMC 100, #18-26
Body: tying thread or buttonhole-twist thread

I like white, red, and dark brown or black for this nymph. I really don't think it is necessary to tie the String Thing, which has the buttonhole-twist thread body. It is very nicely segmented but is also more trouble to tie.

Green Machine (Midge Pupa)

Hook: TMC 100, #22-24
Thread: green
Body: chartreuse flat waxed nylon
Collar: peacock herl
Rib: finest silver wire, three turns

CADDIS IMITATIONS

No-Hackle Caddis

Hook: TMC 100, #18-20
           TMC 2487, #12-18
Thread: brown or tan to match body
Body: hare's ear or other coarse fur, light or dark
Wing: elk hair, well flared

Devil Bug

Hook: TMC 100, #18-20
Thread: brown or tan to match body
Body: hare's ear or other coarse fur or Antron dubbing, light or dark
Wing: brown sparkle yarn, shaped like Humpy body
Shuck: tuft of tan poly dubbing or sparkle yarn

Tie on a pinch of soft poly dubbing at bend of hook and trim to length of hook shank. I prefer Ligas Ultratranslucent nymph dubbing, sand color, to which a tiny amount of orange has been added. Hold a two-inch piece of sparkle yarn (one-ply only) across the bend of the hook. Tie in with figure-eight wraps. Dub body. Comb out sparkle yarn with dubbing needle and pull forward over hook shank. Push sparkle yarn toward rear of hook until Humpy shape is obtained, then hold with left hand while you tie yarn down at front of fly. Stand up yarn with several wraps; whip-finish and cement. Trim yarn to one-third of shank length in front of head.

• Do not put floatant on the shuck when you grease this fly.

    Gary Borger ties this pattern with deer hair, but I prefer this adaptation of his pattern. It works just as well and is much more durable. After I tried this, I came across a stillborn caddis pattern Paul Brown had sketched for me years ago in West Yellowstone. They are virtually identical. Great minds think alike (I wish mine were among them!).

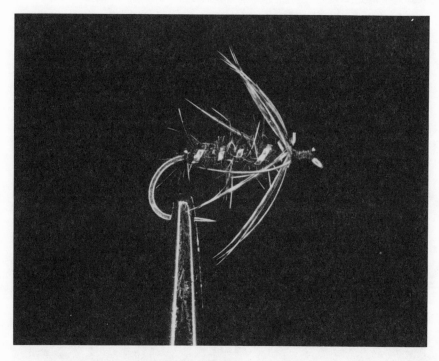

Soft-Hackle Nymph

Hook: TMC 100, #16-20
Thread: brown or tan to match body
Abdomen: hare's ear or other coarse fur or Antron dubbing, light or dark
Rib: fine gold wire, three turns only over abdomen
Thorax: same as abdomen, but prominent and buggy
Hackle: partridge shoulder feather, two turns

Another soft hackle that I really like was shown to me by Bob Giannoni. The Ol' Gray has a gray muskrat abdomen, a dark mink thorax with guard hairs left in, and partridge hackle. It works!

OTHER AQUATICS

Scud

Hook: TMC 2487, #12-18
Thread: orange or tan to match body
Body: mixture of Ligas or fur dubbings in a dubbing loop
Rib: fine copper wire, four turns; or omit
Tails: saddle hackle fibers dyed to match body, or omit

The Orange Scud dubbing is a mixture of equal parts of orange, dirty yellow, and sand Ligas Ultratranslucent nymph dubbing. The Tan Scud uses equal parts of sand and dirty yellow. You may substitute rabbit fur in the same colors and proportions.

Tie rib to shank and wind thread well down onto bend, then back to center of shank. Form a dubbing loop with thread, fill with a generous amount of dubbing, and twist into a buggy chenille. Wrap chenille down to end of body with tying thread, then wind tying thread forward to head. Wrap chenille forward, smoothing fibers back with your left hand after each turn. Tie off and trim. Trim sides and top of fly very close. Wind rib forward, tie off, trim, whip-finish, and cement. Pick out any fibers you may have tied down with the rib.

You will find that this is a more effective fly if you resist the urge to put a plastic shellback on it. We now know that trout chew big bites of food. This fly is very soft and the trout keep it in their mouths longer if it does not have the shellback.

Jim is one of the most gracious fishermen you'll ever meet. He showed me the Orange Scud in May of the first year I attempted to fish the Canyon. He used to fish with his Brittany spaniel. The dog died a few years ago, and we miss having her on the stream. Jim is still there almost every Saturday, often giving up good spots for others to enjoy. The Platte has a lot of fishermen like Jim, but not nearly enough.

San Juan Worm

Hook: Mustad 3906, #14
Thread: to match body
Body: two-inch length of red, brown, or pink ultrachenille, tied to hook in one place only

If you have any comments on this book I would like to hear from you. Write to me at:

445 Wintery Circle South
Colorado Springs, CO 80919

Good luck, good hatches, tight lines.

Index